MONEY

FOUNTAINHEAD PRESS V SERIES

Edited by
Kenneth Gillam

FOUNTAINHEAD
PRESS

Our green initiatives include:

Electronic Products
We deliver products in non-paper form whenever possible. This includes pdf downloadables, flash drives, & CDs.

Electronic Samples
We use Xample, a new electronic sampling system. Instructor samples are sent via a personalized web page that links to pdf downloads.

FSC Certified Printers
All of our printers are certified by the Forest Service Council which promotes environmentally and socially responsible management of the world's forests. This program allows consumer groups, individual consumers, and businesses to work together hand-in-hand to promote responsible use of the world's forests as a renewable and sustainable resource.

Recycled Paper
Most of our products are printed on a minimum of 30% post-consumer waste recycled paper.

Support of Green Causes
When we do print, we donate a portion of our revenue to green causes. Listed below are a few of the organizations that have received donations from Fountainhead Press. We welcome your feedback and suggestions for contributions, as we are always searching for worthy initiatives.
Rainforest 2 Reef
Environmental Working Group

First Edition

ISBN: 978-1-59871-480-7

Printed in the United States of America

INTRODUCTION TO THE FOUNTAINHEAD PRESS V SERIES

By Brooke Rollins and Lee Bauknight
Series Editors

The *Fountainhead Press V Series* is a new collection of single-topic readers that take a unique look at some of today's most pressing issues. Designed to give writing students a more nuanced introduction to public discourse—on the environment, on food, and on digital life, to name a few of the topics—the books feature writing, research, and invention prompts that can be adapted to nearly any kind of college writing class. Each *V Series* textbook focuses on a single issue and includes multi-genre and multimodal readings and assignments that move the discourse beyond the most familiar patterns of debate—patterns usually fettered by entrenched positions and often obsessed with "winning."

The ultimate goal of the series is to help writing students—who tend to hover on the periphery of public discourse—think, explore, find their voices, and skillfully compose texts in a variety of media and genres. Not only do the books help students think about compelling issues and how they might address them, they also give students the practice they need to develop their research, rhetorical, and writing skills. Together, the readings, prompts, and longer assignments show students how to add their voices to the conversations about these issues in meaningful and productive ways.

With enough readings and composing tasks to sustain an entire quarter or semester, and inexpensive enough to be used in combination with other rhetorics and readers, the *Fountainhead Press V Series* provides instructors with the flexibility to build the writing courses they want and need to teach. An instructor interested in deeply exploring environmental issues, for example, could design a semester- or quarter-long course using *Green*, the first of the *V Series* texts. On the other hand, an instructor who wanted to teach discrete units on different issues could use two or more of the *V Series* books. In either case, the texts would give students ample opportunity—and a variety of ways—to engage with the issues at hand.

The *V Series* uses the term "composition" in its broadest sense. Of course, the textbooks provide students plenty of opportunities to write, but they also include assignments that take students beyond the page. Books in the series encourage students to explore other modes of communication by prompting them to design web sites, for example; to produce videos, posters, and presentations; to conduct primary and secondary research; and to develop projects with community partners that might incorporate any number of these skills. Ultimately, we have designed the *Fountainhead Press V Series* to work for teachers and students. With their carefully chosen readings, built-in flexibility, and sound rhetorical grounding, the *V Series* books would be a dynamic and user-friendly addition to any writing class.

TABLE OF CONTENTS

INTRODUCTION: THE MONEY IN YOUR HAND AND THE MONEY IN THE SKY

By Kenneth Gillam

Because that's where the money is.

> —Famous bankrobber "Slick" Willie Sutton after being asked why he robs banks.

You...you're thinking of this place all wrong. As if I had the money back in a safe. The, the money's not here. Well, your money's in Joe's house... that's right next to yours. And in the Kennedy House, and Mrs. Macklin's house, and, and a hundred others.

> —George Bailey, *It's a Wonderful Life*

For the love of money is a root of all kinds of evil.

> —I Timothy 6:10

I got my mind on my money and my money on my mind.

> —Snoop Dogg

Money is something you can hold in your hand. Real, tangible, paper and coins have weight and texture, can jingle in your purse, can get lost or found or cycled through the laundry. Money can burn a hole in your pocket or wait in your piggy bank for a rainy day; you can discover it beneath the couch cushions or stash it in the ash tray of your car. At the same time, and in larger quantities, money is an abstraction, a grand social agreement by which numbers in spreadsheets or information coded on magnetic strips can help us acquire the things we want or need. The money directly deposited by your employer into your checking account, then transferred online to pay your credit card companies for purchases you've charged—we might refer to this as money in the sky. It is real enough—you've earned and spent it—but it never exists anywhere outside a computer or the ether through which information travels in the modern age.

In either form, money at its most basic represents a medium of exchange, a substitute for older forms of trading that allows for an exceedingly complex social system. In simple societies—not just those of the distant past but even, say, the networks between family members and friends—a person might easily trade something they have for something they want without the use of money: if you give me some of that pizza, I'll share my soda. Nor are concrete objects the only barterable items: if you'll critique my essay, I'll water your plants while you're away.

Sumerian stringed shell money

Even in a monetary system, what most of us have to offer is our labor and time, and we exchange those for material goods or for the labor and time of others. Money allows for these exchanges to become more complex than would be possible through simple bartering. Generally shared criteria for determining value ensure that even very different skills and talents can be easily exchanged for goods and services, for instance: a gas station attendant doesn't have to figure out how many gallons to trade for a therapeutic massage, a week of childcare, a Geology textbook, or double bypass surgery. Credit agreements allow larger exchanges to be spread over time or arranged for the future: even someone with no savings might need to get a car, a plane ticket, or a central air conditioning system. And, of course, an extensive legal and governmental apparatus can provide protection to the trading parties, so that no one gets treated unfairly, forbidden from buying or selling, or exploited by those with more leverage in the bargain.

A government's relationship to money is not simply protective, however, and money rises ever more skyward in the workings of our economic institutions. Governments spend money on the things they are obliged or expected to provide for their citizenry—things like education, infrastructure, and law enforcement—and they raise the money to pay for these things not just by taxation but by borrowing, both from their own citizens and from other countries. Taxation seems concrete enough when we mail our checks in April and see the balance in our checking accounts reduced, and when we pay for a treasury bond we receive in return a paper IOU of sorts. But the president of China doesn't hand the American president a briefcase full of cash when we "borrow" from the Chinese economy. Indeed, the very abstract nature of the financial world makes possible a nation-sized budget of deficits, expenditures, and promises. Central banks operate almost exclusively with money in the sky—figuratively, they function as much like a thermostat as anything, making decisions about interest rates, for instance, in order to heat the economy up if it's too cold or cool it down if it's too hot. Their decisions don't always work, and the temperature isn't always comfortable. But successful or not, most of the things governments do with money have little to do with what's printed at the Mint. The money they work with is far, far above your hands.

Our government, of course, isn't alone in this abstract world of money; like the sky, its boundaries extend far past the borders of the United States. Private banks on an international scale, through lending, investing, and trading with one another, exert terrific influence on global finances. Private bankers can manipulate markets, take risky gambles, even directly or indirectly influence governmental policies. In simple terms, the value of money—even that five dollar bill in your pocket—is created and manipulated by people in

Due to hyperinflation, the country of Zimbabwe has had to issue higher and higher denomination notes

whose hands the whole system is entrusted. The things that happen to the economy—a recession, skyrocketing inflation, mortgages becoming harder to qualify for—don't just "happen"; they are not natural disasters. And as much as you might wish to disengage from this vast and perplexing global economy, chances are that the funds you will use to pay for your retirement, your home, even your education are tangled up in it.

The financial crisis that erupted in September 2008 has shown us that there are risks to locating the global economy quite so ethereally. By late 2008, as many have described, Wall Street was operating like a casino. When interest rates were low, people had gotten loans, but the banks who had provided them began to gamble on these promises. They grouped and exchanged them with other banks, betting, raising, bluffing, and hedging their bets with insurance policies provided by other gamblers, everyone hoping to be in the right slot when the wheel stopped spinning. When the bets were called due, it seemed that no one had won, and no one had the money to cover their bets. Essentially playing games on paper, bankers made themselves and their companies tremendous amounts of money for a while, and then they brought the Western world to its knees.

In September 2008, in other words, Americans did not simply experience a system failure wherein the economy crashed like a giant computer. Rather, we suffered the consequences of decisions made by human beings with power over that system on which we all depend. Why did those powerful people make what seem now like such irresponsible choices? That's been the subject of numerous articles, books, and documentary films since 2009. For everything else you can say about money, it also has tremendous influence on the behavior and psychology of people. And through all this maneuvering in the ether of the global economy, there was a lot of money to be made, money that would translate into in-hand salary and bonuses for the bankers at play. Surely, the decisions made by those human beings—like the decisions any of us might make in similar circumstances, perhaps—were influenced by all that money.

The power of money is even more insidious than greed. Money forms the basis of compelling ideological systems, or those sets of beliefs, conscious or otherwise, that we use to ascribe meaning and value to things. Notions of class status, for instance, can provoke or excuse the unequal treatment of groups of people and the expectations we have about them. From the proverbial "in-crowd" of fashionable high schoolers to the Donald Trumps of business and industry, people may believe that they simply deserve better (or worse) lives than others, in terms not only of sustenance, comfort, and fashion but basic human dignity. Definitions of financial "success" may even alter the ways we esteem ourselves. We may blame elite and elitist bankers who seem to have disregarded the value of the common man's money in their pursuit of million-dollar bonuses, but we must be mindful of how money intrinsically influences the rest of us, too. None of us is entirely immune, and the consequences are significant, in large and small ways, for all of us.

Mr. Moneybags from the game Monopoly

Economic ideologies may also drive governmental policy in more subtle ways than the financial meltdown of 2008. Whatever our political or economic philosophy, most of us believe in a social system where at least some money goes to provide things for the public good: things like education, infrastructure, and law enforcement. But ideologies that hold some people more deserving, some more important, and some more expendable than others can extend to the things that government tries to provide to everyone. Capitalism, the economic model that governs most of the Western world, tends to find its ethical code in the wisdom of the market, fair but profitable trade, buying and selling with little external control, and gleaning whatever the market will bear for whatever you have to exchange. We live in a world where a staggeringly unequal distribution of wealth among individuals may be seen as appropriate, as long as the wealth is earned within the ethics of capitalism. But such inequality is often replicated on the entire social structure, so that poorer people get lower-functioning schools, more dangerous neighborhoods, and substandard healthcare. Questions of fairness and ethics quickly become much more complicated.

I would not argue that money is an evil. The oft-misquoted scripture at the beginning of this introduction clearly blames an emotional effusion, not a medium of commercial exchange. And we certainly need money in modern society: we trade it for the food we eat, the electricity that heats and lights our homes, the fuel for our cars. At the same time, though, money—and what we do with it—undeniably shapes our attitudes, reflects our beliefs, and drives our behaviors. What we spend our money on, what we'll do to earn it, and what we are willing to share, have everything to do with the way we value ourselves and our relationships to others. Our financial decisions reflect not simply our preferences but our value systems and ethical codes.

This book offers perspectives on money in many of its manifestations: the tangible, the abstract, the necessary, the luxuriant, the identity-formative, the ethical. There are pieces that discuss having a lot of it and pieces that describe having very little. Included are humor, satire, and lamentation, analyses, explorations, and complaints. I also include a variety of voices with a variety of concerns: as money comes to bear on nearly every field of human inquiry in one form or another, in this volume history, religion, economics, psychology, journalism, literature, and music all speak. These writers explain how money functions, how the middle class has changed over a generation, why college costs so much, and why minimum wage workers can't always just pull themselves up by their bootstraps. Women, Christians, gamers, musicians, and teachers get to frankly confront their value systems and the systems that value them. And cheapskates and spendthrifts both find merit in their philosophies of spending.

These articles, excerpts, songs and images will, I hope, give you a wider perspective on money as an incredibly powerful entity—from the economic systems that make it work, to the social systems that can't work without it, to the people on whom it works its influence. Although the book invites you to learn about and critique the larger systems of money in the sky, it encourages you also to consider how the money in your hand affects you, from your shopping habits and financial planning to your appraisals of yourself and others. Ultimately, even more than the money in your hand or in the sky, this book is about the money on your mind. I hope that you'll ask yourself hard questions as you move through this volume and reflect on your attitudes toward money.

Given the widespread use of things such as direct deposit, debit and credit cards, student loans, tollway passes and the like, how is our relationship to money changing? What is the difference between laying down six $100 bills on the counter for an iPad and paying for it with a credit card? For that matter, when visiting foreign countries, do you notice that it's easier to spend euros, dinars, or yen more easily than U.S. dollars?

On the internet, look at historical and contemporary currencies. What is the relationship between the objects that stand for money and the society that uses those objects?

Take out a $1 bill. Look it over thoroughly and write about what you see. How do the images and iconography relate to you? Does this say anything about how you view your connectedness or disconnectedness from your culture?

Money

Travis McCoy is the vocalist for the group Gym Class Heroes who had a 2006 hit with the song "Cupid's Chokehold." "Billionaire," released in May, 2010 from his solo album Lazarus, went to number four on the Billboard Hot 100 Chart. Of the song, McCoy told MTV News that "It's about what I would do with the money and, at the same time, it opens up the question, if you were in a position to do something with a decent chunk of money, what would you do?"

BILLIONAIRE

BY TRAVIS MCCOY

I wanna be a billionaire so fucking bad,
buy all of the things I never had.
I wanna be on the cover of *Forbes* magazine
smiling next to Oprah and the Queen.

Every time I close my eyes
I see my name in shining lights,
a different city every night.
Oh, I swear the world better prepare
for when I'm a billionaire.

Yeah, I would have a show like Oprah.
I would be the host of everyday Christmas,
give Travie your wish list.
I'd probably pull an Angelina and Brad Pitt
and adopt a bunch of babies that ain't never had shit.
Give away a few Mercedes like, "Here lady have this,"
and last but not least grant somebody their last wish.
It's been a couple months that I've been single so
you can call me Travie Claus minus the *Ho Ho*.
Get it, I'd probably visit where Katrina hit
and damn sure do a lot more than FEMA did.
Yeah, can't forget about me, stupid.
Everywhere I go, I'm'a have my own theme music.

Oh, every time I close my eyes
I see my name in shining lights,
a different city every night.
Oh, I swear the world better prepare
for when I'm a billionaire

I'll be playing basketball with the President,
dunking on his delegates,
then I'll compliment him on his political etiquette.
Toss a couple *milli* in the air just for the heck of it,
but keep the fives, twenties, tens, and Bens completely separate.
And yeah, I'll be in a whole new tax bracket.
We in recession but let me take a crack at it.
I'll probably take whatever's left and just split it up
So everybody that I love can have a couple bucks.
And not a single tummy around me would know what hungry was:
eating good, sleeping soundly.
I know we all have a similar dream.
Go in your pocket, pull out your wallet,
and put it in the air and sing.

I wanna be a billionaire so fucking bad,
buy all of the things I never had.
I wanna be on the cover of *Forbes* magazine
smiling next to Oprah and the Queen.

McCoy expresses an altruistic urge in this song; he sings about how he will help people with his newfound wealth. Research local charities and settle on one that you think would have the greatest impact on your community if you were to suddenly become a billionaire with money to give away. Why would this charity be more helpful than others and how much would you give?

Throughout human history there has been a tension between being selfish and being selfless. Many religious texts directly address this conundrum and generally err on the side of selflessness and altruism. McCoy seems to want to have it both ways: to be both selfish and selfless (or at least helpful to his family and friends). Write a journal or blog entry in which you explore this tension within yourself.

Read Scalzi's "Being Poor" on page 89. In a group, write out a list beginning each line: "Being rich means…"

MONEY

Founded at University of Wisconsin-Madison in 1988 by Tim Keck and Christopher Johnson and subsequently run by Scott Dikkers, The Onion is a satirical newspaper and website that sends up local, national, and international news. Although satirical and parodic, from time to time The Onion's "news stories" have been reported as fact by such regular news outlets as the New York Times and The Fox Nation.

U.S. ECONOMY GRINDS TO A HALT AS NATION REALIZES MONEY JUST A SYMBOLIC, MUTUALLY SHARED ILLUSION

THE ONION

Washington—The U.S. economy ceased to function this week after unexpected existential remarks by Federal Reserve chairman Ben Bernanke shocked Americans into realizing that money is, in fact, just a meaningless and intangible social construct.

Calling it "basically no more than five rectangular strips of paper," Fed chairman Ben Bernanke illustrates how much "$200" is actually worth.

What began as a routine report before the Senate Finance Committee Tuesday ended with Bernanke passionately disavowing the entire concept of currency, and negating in an instant the very foundation of the world's largest economy.

"Though raising interest rates is unlikely at the moment, the Fed will of course act appropriately if we…if we…" said Bernanke, who then paused for a moment, looked down at his prepared statement, and shook his head in utter disbelief. "You know what? It doesn't matter. None of this—this so-called 'money'—really matters at all."

"It's just an illusion," a wide-eyed Bernanke added as he removed bills from his wallet and slowly spread them out before him. "Just look at it: Meaningless pieces of paper with numbers printed on them. Worthless."

According to witnesses, Finance Committee members sat in thunderstruck silence for several moments until Sen. Orrin Hatch (R-UT) finally shouted out, "Oh my God, he's right. It's all a mirage. All of it—the money, our whole economy—it's all a lie!'"

Screams then filled the Senate Chamber as lawmakers and members of the press ran for the exits, leaving in their wake aisles littered with the remains of torn currency. U.S. markets closed as traders left their jobs and resolved for once to do or make something, anything of real value.

As news of the nation's collectively held delusion spread, the economy ground to a halt, with dumbfounded citizens everywhere walking out on their jobs as they contemplated the little green drawings of buildings and dead white men they once used to measure their adequacy and importance as human beings.

At the New York Stock Exchange, Wednesday morning's opening bell echoed across a silent floor as the few traders who arrived for work out of habit looked up blankly at the meaningless scrolling numbers on the flashing screens above.

"I've spent 25 years in this room yelling 'Buy, buy! Sell, sell!' and for what?" longtime trader Michael Palermo said. "All I've done is move arbitrary designations of wealth from one column to another, wasting my life chasing this unattainable hallucination of wealth."

"What a cruel cosmic joke," he added. "I'm going home to hug my daughter."

Sources at the White House said President Obama was "still trying to get his head around all this" and was in seclusion with his coin collection, muttering "it's just metal, it's just metal" over and over again.

"The president will be making a statement very soon," press secretary Robert Gibbs told reporters. "At the moment, though, his mind is just too blown to comment."

A few U.S. banks have remained open, though most teller windows are unmanned due to a lack of interest in transactions involving mere scraps of paper or, worse, decimal points and computer data signifying mere scraps of paper. At a Bank of America branch in Spokane, WA, curious former customers wandered aimlessly through a large empty vault, while several would-be robbers of a Chase bank in Columbus, OH reportedly put their guns down and exited the building hand in hand with security guards, laughing over the inherent absurdity of the idea of $100 bills.

Likewise, the real estate industry has all but vanished, with mortgage lenders seeing no reason to stop people from reclaiming their foreclosed-upon homes.

"I don't even know what we were thinking in the first place," said former banker Nathan Collins of Brandon, MS, as he jimmyed open a door to allow a single mother and her five children to move back into their house. "A bunch of people sign a bunch of papers, and now this family has no place to live? That's just plain ludicrous."

The realization that money is nothing more than an elaborate head game seems to have penetrated the entire country: In Wilmington, DE, for instance, a collection agent reportedly broke down in joyful sobs when he informed a woman on the other end of the phone that he had absolutely no reason to harass her anymore, as her Discover Card debt was no longer comprehensible.

For some Americans, the fog of disbelief surrounding the nation's epiphany has begun to lift, with many building new lives free from the illusion of money.

"It's back to basics for me," Bernard Polk of Waverly, OH said. "I'm going to till the soil for my own sustenance and get anything else I need by bartering. If I want milk, I'll pay for it in tomatoes. If need a new hoe, I'll pay for it in lettuce."

When asked, hypothetically, how he would pay for complicated life-saving surgery for a loved one, Polk seemed uncertain.

"That's a lot of vegetables, isn't it?" he said.

Using a reference book or the web, find definitions of "satire" and "comedy." This piece is clearly intended to be funny—is it also satire? What, if anything, is being satirized? What, if anything, is the grain of truth underneath the humor? Consider the excerpt from *Catch-22* (page 157) and how these two pieces are rhetorically similar.

The article claims that money is "meaningless and intangible...an elaborate head game." How are these two adjectives related? Can something be intangible without being meaningless? The two non-celebrity quotes in the article—trader Michael Palermo and Bernard Polk of Waverly, Ohio—give examples of the way people tend to see money in context or in competition with other things of value from familial love to healthcare. Write a paragraph in which you analyze your own concept of value: How do you think about money (or other prized possessions), and what standards do you use for assessing the value of the things around you?

Imagine that when you wake up tomorrow, money as we know it has disappeared, though everything else (so far) remains operable. If we started all over, what would give things value? What would a Picasso original be worth? What about a pound of ground beef? Stock in Microsoft? Diamonds? Clean water? In your small group, make a list of things you think would hold their value and discuss why you think so?

The 32nd president of the United States, Franklin Delano Roosevelt, was elected to serve four terms between 1933 and 1945. He died nearing the end of his fourth term during the waning days of World War II. FDR was elected during the Great Depression and instituted a host of social and economic programs he termed the New Deal. Some of these programs, Social Security and the Federal Deposit Insurance Corporation (FDIC) are still in existence. FDR placed blame for the Great Depression squarely on the shoulders of bankers and financiers and much of the New Deal was aimed at relieving unemployment, restarting the economy, and fixing the problems that led to the crisis in the first place. The following is an excerpt from his 1944 State of the Union Address.

excerpt from

THE ECONOMIC BILL OF RIGHTS

BY FRANKLIN DELANO ROOSEVELT

[…] We have come to a clear realization of the fact that true individual freedom cannot exist without economic security and independence. "Necessitous men are not free men." People who are hungry and out of a job are the stuff of which dictatorships are made.

In our day these economic truths have become accepted as self-evident. We have accepted, so to speak, a second Bill of Rights under which a new basis of security and prosperity can be established for all—regardless of station, race, or creed.

Among these are:

The right to a useful and remunerative job in the industries or shops or farms or mines of the Nation;

The right to earn enough to provide adequate food and clothing and recreation;

The right of every farmer to raise and sell his products at a return which will give him and his family a decent living;

The right of every businessman, large and small, to trade in an atmosphere of freedom from unfair competition and domination by monopolies at home or abroad;

The right of every family to a decent home;

The right to adequate medical care and the opportunity to achieve and enjoy good health;

The right to adequate protection from the economic fears of old age, sickness, accident, and unemployment;

The right to a good education.

All of these rights spell security. And after this war is won we must be prepared to move forward, in the implementation of these rights, to new goals of human happiness and well-being. **[…]**

Excerpt from President Roosevelt's January 11, 1944 message to the Congress of the United States on the State of the Union.

Consider this speech in its historical context: the two things most pressing on the American imagination in 1944 were, doubtless, the Great Depression and WWII. Do any of FDR's stated "rights" seem historically contingent? Which ones, and why? Should FDR have stated these ideals as the rights of American citizens? How does the recent congressional debate over health care coverage reflect the ways in which this conversation has continued into the present?

Do you think any economic ideals should be guaranteed by the American government to its citizens? Are there things on this list that you think should be removed? If so, why? Are there things that you think should be added to this list as "rights" enjoyed by all Americans? What would your "economic bill of rights" look like?

FDR states that poverty and unemployment are "the stuff of which dictatorships are made." Consider this claim and the argument that these ideals are not just rights humans deserve but are steps toward political security. Have you witnessed or experienced a situation in which need seems to conflict with peace or freedom? Write a description of the conflict as well as the way the situation was resolved. What would it take for that resolution to apply across a whole nation? Would that situation provide an appropriate parallel?

Writer MP Dunleavey writes the "Cost of Living" column for the New York Times, the "Financial Balance" column for Body & Soul, and "Ask MP" for Parenting magazine. Her advice columns garner thousands upon thousands of readers each month. "Buy Yourself Less Stuff" is an excerpt from her 2007 book, Money Can Buy Happiness.

BUY YOURSELF LESS STUFF

By MP Dunleavey

The world is too much with us; late and soon,
Getting and spending, we lay waste our powers.

—William Wordsworth

We humans seem to suffer from a fundamental flaw when it comes to making a connection between money and happiness. The problem doesn't arise so much with the things we buy, but with our expectations for the extent to which material goods can really improve our quality of life.

Many years ago, Steve, now sixty, was a lieutenant in the army, stationed on the West Coast with his wife and baby daughter. Life was good, but he knew one thing would make it perfect: a Jaguar XKE—"the most beautiful production car ever made," he says. "I always thought, 'If only I could have an XKE, it would make me so happy!' So finally I said, damn, I'm going to buy me a Jaguar."

He couldn't afford to buy one, so he set his sights on finding the most perfect "pre-owned" XKE that he could. Steve remembers poring over the classified ads until he found the right one, and he paid about $2,500 for it—a huge sum in those days. At first it was everything he'd dreamed of: sleek, classy, and luxurious. He really couldn't have been a happier guy. Wife, daughter, Jaguar XKE—what more does a man need from life? But soon the joy began to ebb. In fact, he says, "That car made me miserable. It was temperamental and high-maintenance, and as soon as you'd fix one thing another thing would break."

The constant maintenance wore on his nerves and strained his marriage. (One low point, he says, was when his wife found him obsessively scrubbing the hubcaps in the bathtub.) But it wasn't the upkeep that was such a letdown, but that such a major purchase could be so disappointing. It was a huge financial investment that didn't yield the kind of ongoing golden glow of satisfaction he'd assumed it would. Finally, he sold the Jaguar and faced a lesson he never forgot. "It taught me that things *really* don't make you happy," Steve says.

I doubt you're surprised by Steve's revelation; most people could have told him before he bought the car that it would brighten his life by only so much. Yet no matter how often we remind ourselves—"Hey, that new car/stereo/granite countertop is going to make me only so happy"—it doesn't seem to diminish the constant craving so many of us have for bigger, better, shinier, faster, more high-tech stuff. Or the fantasy that somewhere up the chain of purchases, you'll hit the one that finally completes you.

Perhaps you're one of those enlightened souls who has already put materialism in perspective. If so, I salute you—but as a fellow consumer, I'm also a little skeptical. Here's why.

Nearly forty years ago, Richard Easterlin, now an economist at the University of Southern California, began examining people's material desires and how they felt once they achieved those goals. Easterlin reviewed surveys of thousands of Americans, who said they believed the good life consisted of owning certain things—like having a nice car, pool, vacation home, and so one. While they themselves had only 1.7 of the desired items, they felt that owning 4.4 (on average) would constitute a satisfactory life.

That seems reasonable. You don't quite have all the things you want, but you're sure that when you acquire them, you'll be satisfied.

But when Easterlin then studied people's responses to the same questions many years later, he found that although on average people now owned 3.1 of the desired goods—now they believed they wouldn't achieve the so-called good life until they owned 5.6 of them.

You can see how the underlying itch to acquire more (and more) turns into a never-ending treadmill of consumption—not because the things we want are bad, but because we attach to them an impossible outcome: that certain possessions can and will increase our happiness.

The confounding factor is that owning and buying stuff actually *is* fun. It's a normal, natural part of life—one of the perks of having to spend your allotted time on planet earth. But a problem unfolds when the momentary kick fades, and your natural instinct is to want to achieve that feel-good state again somehow. So you strive for the next thing, in the belief that maybe if you get more bang for your buck, this time it will last.

> *After a time, you may find that having is not so pleasing a thing, after all, as wanting. It is not logical, but it is often true.*
>
> —Mr. Spock

Unfortunately, a buck can buy only so much bang, and very quickly you're caught on what researchers have dubbed the "hedonic treadmill," the ceaseless quest of *moremoremore* that drives our lives, dominates our thoughts, and erodes our quality of life.

THE GRASS IS ALWAYS GREENER

Why? Because people have an astonishing ability to adapt to almost any circumstance, positive or negative, with little change in our overall sense of well-being. Even studies of cancer patients and paraplegics have shown that people whom most of us would imagine to be depressed or suffering actually report being about as happy as healthy folks—because they've adapted to their lives. To be sure, a calamity like a sudden death, divorce, or job loss can be traumatic and isn't something you just adjust to quickly at all. But the bulk of human experiences, *especially when it comes to most monetary or material gains*, have a surprisingly short-lived effect on how happy you are.

Alas, that's not what most of us believe. You may have felt the whirring of that treadmill underfoot after a Saturday shopping at the mall, or when you finished renovating the kitchen or splurged on a hand-tailored suit or an expensive new watch. It's not that those things didn't bring you pleasure. You were probably thrilled at first. It's just that within a fairly short time the excitement fades. Life returns to normal. You still squabble with your mate.

Your boss is a pain. You haven't lost that five pounds. So you start looking for the next big thrill—and back on the treadmill you go.

I remember when I was earning $18,000 a year, in my first job after college. If only I could make $35,000, I recall telling a friend, I would be totally happy— I'd have everything I needed.

A few years later, when I was making $35,000 a year, I realized all I needed was an income of $50,000. That seemed reasonable. Life was so hard on a mere $35,000. Get me $15,000 more and my problems would vanish!

Then, when I was making $50,000 (this all really happened), it was clear to me: I needed to make at least $80,000 to be okay, but $100,000—that magic six-figure number—was what it would take to *truly* give me the life I wanted, shore up my insecurities, and finally vanquish any and all lingering problems.

The never-ending upward spiral seems clear now, and yet it took me years to see that I was caught in the Must Have More cycle that defines modern life.

THE UNDERLYING POWER OF MONEY

So how do you get off the hamster wheel of "getting and spending" in order to invest in a happier way of life? These choices don't happen overnight. You can't call your happiness broker at Merrill Lynch and say, "Get me some shares of happiness, and sell this treadmill stuff, will ya? It's going nowhere." If only it were that simple.

In order to shift your focus away from stuff in order to invest more in life, it helps to understand some of the powerful dynamics, both internal and external, that may be influencing how and why you invest your financial resources.

MONEY AND THE BRAIN

Some scientists have speculated that the acquisition of money and things creates a kind of dopamine rush in the brain, similar to addiction, which may be one reason why it's hard for people to stop chasing after material thrills. Others have pointed out that human beings are hardwired, from an evolutionary perspective, to compete for the best and most of any goods available. This "keeping up with the Joneses" that we all know and dread thus contributes to what Harvard psychologist Daniel Gilbert has called "the cycle of miswanting," because people feel compelled to invest in the things that won't make them happy instead of the things that do.

MONEY AND COMPETITION

Most people are striving to find that balance, but as we all know it's a constant struggle—and it's not new. With the publication of *The Theory of the Leisure Class* in 1899, economist Thorstein Veblen coined the term "conspicuous consumption" to describe a phenomenon that will sound as contemporary as *InStyle* magazine. Conspicuous consumption is not about buying things you need, but about buying things as a symbol of your earning power, a signal to others that you've attained a certain level of wealth. These days conspicuous consumption has escalated into an even more aggressive form of one-upmanship that some call "competitive consumption." That's the desire to have things that not only display your purchasing power, but your ability to outstrip whatever your neighbor just acquired.

MATERIALISM AND YOUR NEIGHBOR

As I mentioned in the last chapter, we are all vulnerable to the financial and material influences of the environment in which we live—never mind the pervasive power of media and advertising. But as much as you want to believe you're in charge of your own behavior, it pays to be aware of the impact that others' behavior may have on your own "investment" decisions, whether you know it or not.

> *Never keep up with the Joneses. Drag them down to your level. It's cheaper.*
>
> —Quentin Crisp

This was captured in an article I read about the phenomenon of automaticity—the fascinating and depressing human tendency to imitate what's going on around us. One study found that when people were told to complete a task next to an experimenter who, for example, often rubbed her face, subjects like-wise tended to rub their faces, even though afterward they had no idea that the experimenter's fidgeting had been "contagious." Another study found that when people were merely shown a series of words associated with being elderly, they behaved in a more elderly manner (i.e., walked slower, were more forgetful)—again, without realizing they had succumbed to a series of covert directions, if you will.

It's not hard to imagine, then, the impact on your own financial desires when a friend spends twenty minutes relating her latest shopping extravaganza, describing her new Bose stereo, or has you take a spin in her cute new customized, fully loaded Mini Cooper.

INFLATION OF OUR EXPECTATIONS

So although it may seem obvious that buying less stuff will provide you with extra resources to invest in a happier way of life, every day you have to fend off a series of stealth assaults on your financial sanity—including the steady inflation of your own expectations for what a so-called "normal" or "average" life consists of.

Witness the average size of a new single-family home. In the early 1970s it was 1,500 square feet. As of early 2005 the average home size had grown to 2,400 square feet—and with it, people's expectations of how big an "average" home should be as well as which amenities should come with it, says Gopal Ahluwalia, vice president of research for the National Association of Home Builders.

What was once considered upscale is now the "new normal" for homeowners today, Ahluwalia says: from his and hers walk-in closets in the master bedroom to kitchen islands with cooktops to three-car garages. (People don't want a three-car garage because they have three cars, he added, but because they want to make sure they have enough storage for all their excess stuff.)

Nor have home sizes increased because people have bigger families. In the last thirty-five years, Ahluwalia says, the average family size declined to 2.11 people from 3.58.

That hasn't stopped people from spending a lot more money for an expanded way of life—whether or not they can afford it. No wonder Americans are experiencing an epidemic of debt and bankruptcy, the likes of which has never been seen before.

IF ONLY BIGGER WAS ALWAYS BETTER

How do you combat the multitude of forces that influence how you spend your money and live your life? The first step is to become better acquainted with the joys of "inconspicuous consumption."

Inconspicuous consumption doesn't get a lot of airtime; you can't get it on sale at Kmart; Wal-Mart doesn't carry big tubs of it at a discount. The less-tangible pleasures in life rarely have the same wow power as things, even though they are more deeply satisfying. The core assets in the happiness portfolio I outlined in the last chapter are all based on inconspicuous consumption—spending less on stuff and more on life.

EXERCISE
Your Money and/or Your Life

To illustrate the contrast between conspicuous material desires and inconspicuous ones, Cornell economist Robert Frank created a series of thought experiments (below). The questions are based on his model, which you can find in his excellent book about the escalating insanity of materialism, *Luxury Fever.* There are no right answers—just read each one and think about it.

1. If you could live in a 4,000-square-foot home and have one week of vacation a year, or live in a 2,000-square-foot home and have three weeks' vacation, which would you choose?

2. If you could have a job that paid $200,000 a year, but you could only see your friends once a month, vs. a job that paid $100,000 and you could see your friends every week—which would you choose?

3. If you could buy a new 3,000-square-foot house for $400,000 (incurring a hefty mortgage) or an older home of the same size that would require some work for $200,000 (and more affordable monthly payments), which would you choose?

4. If you could land a job at the top of your profession, but you got to see your children for only a handful of hours a week, vs. keeping a job with less prestige, but which gave you a flexible schedule—which would you choose?

I love these brain twisters because they're a potent reminder that many of the assumptions we all live with—that the bigger house or better job is always the more desirable choice—may not be deep down what we all want at all. In fact, it would be wise to consider whether choosing the alternatives might be the high road to a much more satisfying quality of life.

A few years ago, Kurt and Diane, a couple in their thirties, seemed like poster children for conspicuous consumption—from their four-bedroom house in a nice suburb of Chicago to their shiny Subaru.

But they weren't happy. They both missed living in the city, where they'd gone to college (and where many of their friends still lived). They found caring for their big house and yard a drag; Kurt hated his long commute. So they did the opposite of what many people aspire to: They sold their house, sold their car, and moved back to the city. "We never felt comfortable living in that house," Diane admits. "It wasn't the life we wanted at all. It was too isolated. And what did we need all that space for?" Come to find out, spending their money on a less conspicuous home in a more culture-rich, friend-centric city held the most meaning for them.

Kurt and Diane didn't end up living frugally on a farm somewhere—they would have been miserable. In fact, they didn't end up spending any less money. But they did decide to invest their money in less conspicuous ways that would make them conspicuously happier.

Instead of an hour-long commute to and from work, it now takes Kurt fifteen minutes to get to the office, so he has more time to focus on his side business in graphic design and hang out with the family. Their son's preschool is within walking distance of their home, so they can take turns walking him to school. If they need a car, they rent one. The couple has easy access to restaurants, museums, countless cultural events, and they can see their friends more often.

That's inconspicuous consumption—and for the most part that's what your happiness portfolio is based on. The key financial principle here is buying less stuff so you can invest in the more durable pleasures of life. But in order to do so, you need to put your personal finance cap on, because the next step requires you to start taking the reins of your financial life by learning where your money goes—and then deciding if that's where you really want it to go.

FOLLOW THE MONEY: YOU'LL BE GLAD YOU DID

In my experience, many people—even some quite successful people—have only a vague idea about where their money goes on a daily, monthly, or yearly basis. And most people hate keeping a so-called spending diary to monitor their expenditures, in part because it's tedious, but mainly because they're afraid of what they'll find.

But the reality is that if you want to upgrade your quality of life, you're going to need to take control over your money to do it—so some sort of overview is needed. So let's make it simple: Rather than asking you to keep a diary of what you spend, I'd like you to keep a record of whether what you spend is being invested in the pursuit of happiness.

In many ways using financial software is the fastest way to track where your money goes. I've used software and found it extremely useful—and these days programs like Excel, Quicken, and Money are easier to use than ever.

> *Money is like an arm or a leg—use it or lose it.*
>
> —Henry Ford, interview with
> the *New York Times*, November 8, 1931

If you have the patience, another money-tracking method is to read through your credit card and bank statements, reviewing every bill paid, every credit and debit purchase (although this won't tell you where that hundred-dollar ATM cash withdrawal went.)

For me, nothing beats carrying around an envelope in your purse, briefcase, or backpack into which you put every single last receipt you get, every day, for a month. Keep a pen handy so you can jot down random items for which you don't have a receipt, like bills you pay or your monthly commuting pass or the seventy-five cents you put in a parking meter.

You also can do some combination of the above: Use software (Money, Excel, Quicken) for all bank transactions; use the envelope to track cash; double-check your statements. Or if little pieces of paper drive you nuts, just keep a detailed spending notebook and forget the receipts. The point is, do whatever works for you, but find a way to monitor how and why and where your money goes for at least two weeks.

Three points:

1. You're not doing this to feel guilty about how much you spend on cigarettes or DVDs or the fact that you got another late charge on your credit card. You're doing this because you want to take control over your money in order to enjoy your life to the hilt.

2. Do this exercise with a friend, otherwise you are likely to crap out—as is only human.

3. Expect yourself to have trouble at first. As with taking up exercise or quitting smoking, you may need a few tries. Don't sweat it. Few people like to do this and even fewer stick to it. Just try. Take a break if you get sick of it. Then try again next week. It's a good idea to attempt this exercise a couple of times a year anyway while you're reorganizing your financial closets. It keeps you focused on your greater goals.

Now, make a list of recent expenses on the worksheet here, and note whether each one has increased your happiness dividends—and if so, in what way. Here is a sample:

EXPENSE	COST	HAPPINESS PORTFOLIO?		HOW?
cell phone	$75	Yes	No ☑	
mortgage	$1,179	Yes ☑	No	security; equity
lunch/week	$47	Yes	No ☑	
Netflix	$9.95	Yes ☑	No	love movies!
gym fee	$89	Yes ☑	No	health, energy, sanity
new shoes	$68	Yes	No ☑	
savings	$200	Yes ☑	No	emergency cushion
plane ticket	$368	Yes ☑	No	visiting best friend

As you can see now, the point is not self-torture, but clarity. This book is about setting priorities, and when you live and spend contrary to what you value— you don't end up with the life you want.

A mundane example is what happens to a lot of people when they go into CVS, Duane Reade, Walgreens, or some other convenience store. You go in wanting toothpaste, and you leave having spent thirty dollars on half a dozen other things. (I've often wondered what happens to us in those stores. Are we overcome by the desperate need for cold medicine and hair conditioner? Supersize bags of Pepperidge Farm Goldfish?)

Anyway, thirty bucks may not seem like a big deal, but what's significant is how easy it is to spend money on lots of stuff... but nothing in particular. Clarifying where your money goes each month not only illuminates these financial black holes so you can retrieve your runaway cash, it also allows you to use that money to make happier choices. Just as you can spend money in such a way that it keeps you jogging on the competitive consumption treadmill, you can use your money to buy your way off it by investing in the things that enhance quality of life: your relationships, your health and well-being, new and stimulating experiences.

Explore

Dunleavey lists four thought experiments created by Robert Frank that force a person to choose between two hypothetical economic scenarios. What do you think the happiest people you know would say if confronted with each question? Ask them. Do your values seem in sync with theirs? Why or why not?

Invent

Consider the items listed in Dunleavey's sample "happiness portfolio" on the preceding page. What are the foundations of your happiness? Which of them are linked to money (security, for instance, might be), and which aren't? What, if anything, does Dunleavey miss in her description of "happiness dividends"?

Compose

In a paragraph, reflect on a time you or someone you know has been caught up in "the cycle of miswanting" (page 22). What motivated or compelled you? What did you want, and did you ultimately buy it? What, if anything, did you learn from the experience?

Collaborate

In a small group, compare your cell phones. What are the features you collectively enjoy? How much do they cost, on a monthly basis? Are they worth it, or are you on some sort of "hedonic treadmill" (page 21)? Why or why not? Add together your cell phone plan monthly costs. What else would that money buy?

Money

Liz Perle is co-founder and editor-in-chief of Common Sense Media, *a not-for-profit site that provides information about media for parents and families. Previously, she worked for many years in the publishing industry for houses such as William Morrow/Avon, Prentice Hall, and Bantam. She is the author of two books:* When Work Doesn't Work Anymore: Women, Work, and Identity *and* Money, A Memoir: Women, Emotions, and Cash, *from which the following is excerpted.*

excerpt from
MONEY: A MEMOIR

By Liz Perle

Somewhere over the Pacific Ocean, I realized I'd better count my money. There'd been no time in the airport. I'd been too busy wrangling a four-year-old and wrestling with my own mix of numbness, efficiency, and sorrow. I'd checked my luggage—a box of toys, a suitcase filled with tropical clothes— and turned to see my husband kneeling by his boy, both of them in tears. My son and I were leaving Singapore, where we'd moved five weeks earlier from New York City to join my husband. He'd been working there for six months. But by the time we'd arrived, he'd changed his mind about wanting to be married.

"Please go home," he said, concluding a tearful discussion we'd had during my first week.

I pointed out that this would be tough since we'd sold our apartment, expecting we'd be in Asia for three years.

"Go. Please," he repeated.

Four weeks later, having exhausted any hope of salvaging our marriage, I stood listing against the Singapore Airlines counter as everyone around me scurried purposefully to somewhere or away from someone. I was having trouble focusing on what was happening. In one hand, I clutched two passports, and in the other, a fistful of bills that had been peeled from a thick wad. Snapping to, I stuffed them in my pocket and took my son in hand, pausing before my husband. Do we hug? Kiss? There was no way for our bodies to say goodbye. I mumbled that I'd call from San Francisco when I got to my friend Sue's house, and headed down the gangway to the waiting plane, tugging my bewildered child.

There were fifteen $100 bills.

I had just lost my marriage and my home, and I had fifteen hundred bucks.

Suffice it to say that the first thing on my mind as I flew thirty-five thousand feet over Guam while headed back to the States was not cash. But putting heartbreak aside, I did have a few concerns: My companion was a four-year-old, I was unemployed, there was no place called home, and every single household possession I owned was in a sealed container on a huge cargo ship steaming its way toward Asia through the Suez Canal.

For as long as I could remember, I'd lived with a kind of chronic anxiety that something like this would happen. That I'd lose my financial footing and end up shuffling around in bedroom slippers pushing a shopping cart down an alley. On the surface of it, this was not a rational fear. Since I was born a relatively middle-to-upper-middle-class girl with all the privileges, experiences, and options that come with membership in the Club of Disposable Income, the chances of my remaining in one end or another of that income bracket were probably going to be pretty good. (That and the fact that, in my saner moments, I did know that my husband was an unhappily married—not bad—man and that he would not leave me and his son high and dry.) But that hadn't stopped me from worrying that one day, without warning, I could plunge from the safety of my nice life into—if not poverty—a quality of life so diminished that I wouldn't be able to bear it. These stubborn fears had persisted through years of economic independence, and they regularly woke me up at 4:00 A.M. disguised as regret over an unnecessary impulse purchase, sure that it represented the first step on the steep path to sheer ruin.

Then, one day, quite suddenly, my worst fears were realized. Without warning, my marriage collapsed, taking with it my financial security. After all, I had (quite willingly) handed over my economic life to my husband. Now he and all our assets were retreating at five hundred miles an hour.

Here's what was clear: that I wasn't getting my marriage back.

Here's what was not so clear: how I was going to afford my life.

There's nothing like losing just about everything to lay bare what's important.

Long ago, and not entirely consciously, I made a quiet contract with cash. I would do what it took to get it—work hard, marry right—but I didn't want to have to think about it. I simply wanted to know I would be financially secure. This intentional avoidance eventually exacted its price. In the service of sidestepping, whenever possible, my anxious feelings (if not my facts) about money, I've signed over a lot of power to anyone or anything that promised to make me feel financially safe—no matter what the consequences. I've left my emotions about money—the fears and ambivalences—largely unexamined. I've avoided facing my contradictory feelings about the whole subject, such as the fact that I want to have my own money with the independence it gives, while simultaneously hoping someone or something will step up to the plate and take care of me. I've invited these highly emotional and unstable sets of feelings into every relationship I've had, and they have silently accompanied and influenced each one—with my father, my work, my friends, my bosses, and my husbands. (There have been two—oddly, both named Steve.)

My nonspecific fears of financial ruin have led to some good things, too, though. They've pushed me to work hard, which propelled me into some good jobs, which, in addition to nice salaries, gave me a sense of identity, some freedom, and extended periods when I felt pretty good about myself. Anxiety about my future has put money in my IRA, has helped me save enough for a down payment on a house, and, in the hopes that the sins of the parents aren't visited on the kids, has prodded me to impart to my children a respect for cash and a sense of its importance. In fact, I've always paid my way, not just out of financial need but because emotionally I've needed the freedom that decent income ensured me.

None of these facts, however, made a dent in my anxieties.

My financial solvency—like most things in life—has come with a few strings attached. In order to keep the real and imaginary wolves from my door, I've occasionally acted in ways that haven't made me feel too swell about myself. I've been silent when I should have spoken up. Stayed ignorant when I should have paid attention. I've remained tethered to unhappy and unhealthy work and personal relationships. I've been complicit in bad business practices and poor management.

My agreement to trade bits of myself for security has had personal side effects—eruptions of rebellious immaturity where I haven't paid my bills or lived within my means in spite of very real consequences. I didn't change my IRA portfolio from all those tech stocks I'd invested in hoping to get rich quick (whoops). I didn't balance my checkbook and ended up paying 18 percent interest on the overdraft that bounced over to my Visa card. I've left jobs purely because I've hated them, even though they paid me well. Each of these incidents resulted in big reversals in my financial fortunes, and if you graphed my net worth over the course of my life, it would look like the mark of Zorro. Embarrassed and occasionally unnerved by my own tendency toward erratic fiscal behavior, I've stubbornly refused to examine it, instead choosing to pin my hopes on that white knight, dream job, unknown dead rich uncle, or winning lottery number that would rescue me.

This kind of magical thinking—if not downright denial—has allowed me to maintain a remarkably constant approach/avoidance relationship with this most fundamental part of my life—with the emphasis on avoidance. I'm no stranger to the financial fantasy realm. My daydreaming drew heavily and rather unimaginatively on the run-of-the-mill Disney model. It involved the acquisition of a husband who would present me with a "happily-ever-after" life by taking away my money fears. Yet despite my most strenuous efforts, I didn't manage to find one until my midthirties. Buried inside my increasingly frantic search for the he-who-would-be-solvent was the fantasy that once married, I would have the security I craved. Insistent feminist that I was (and remain), I still wanted the option of knowing that I, alone, would not have to be the steward of my financial destiny.

I married the first guy I dated who owned a really good suit. (Okay, to be honest, I also married the first guy who asked.) He was handsome and powerful and had an impressive job. He also made more money than I did, which I admit was a total turn-on. (Well, he had some debts and some overvalued real estate. But I overlooked these departures from the script.) On our first date, he told me to get out of the street and go stand on the curb, that he could hail us a cab. He was an alpha male, a self-made man, and clearly comfortable with finance and investment. I exhaled.

In spite of years of paying my own way, I couldn't hand over the checkbook fast enough. He liked to control the cash, pay the bills, invest the money, and govern the expenses. That was more than fine with me. I had a little money in my IRA, a bit more in a 401(k), and some profits from selling a home I'd bought with a small inheritance from my grandmother. We both had good jobs; we both made good money. He managed it. I spent it. That worked for me. I settled into domestic life all too happy to place my financial future in the hands of someone who would show his love for me by paying for everything.

The dream took some unexpected turns—the first being a period when I was out of work. The balance of power shifted quickly, almost toppling our marriage then and there. But when I found a new job with an even better salary than before, things seemed to even out. But then my husband's company reorganized dramatically as it prepared to go public. He'd worked for this firm for twenty-plus years and had many stock options that would be worth a substantial payout if he stayed on. The only hitch was that continued employment meant we'd have to move to Singapore for three years. Since I now had what I craved—a child and financial security—it only seemed fair to support my husband's part of the dream, which involved early retirement, golf, and general relaxation.

I swallowed hard and painted a pretty picture for myself of a life of adventure. I couldn't have a traditional job in Singapore (there was no way I would get a work permit), so instead I looked forward to reading the classics, settling into a routine as a full-time mom, traveling, and writing. Except for that earlier three-month period of unemployment, I had never depended on someone else for money, so a part of me wasn't keen on a repeat performance. But there weren't a lot of options, and I figured the dependency wasn't for too long. I trusted that at the end of the trip, we'd have enough money for my husband to do what he wanted, and for me to feel secure. I was more than willing to trade three years of ungovernably frizzy hair on the humid equator for a lifetime of financial ease. My husband transferred our finances, we sold our home, and after a six-month separation—he'd had to move earlier than I could—my son and I packed that box of toys and suitcase full of shorts and T-shirts, and we moved to Singapore.

We already know how that turned out.

So it was that five weeks later, at the age of forty-two, I bumped down on the stormy tarmac of San Francisco International Airport with no job, no home, and no clue what was going to happen. I had those hundred-dollar bills and, as it turned out, a small savings account, but almost everything else—even the joint credit card I carried—was in my husband's name and under his control half a world away.

This could have been my Scarlett O'Hara moment when I turned draperies into finery and pulled my metaphoric carrots from the earth, proclaiming, "I'll never be hungry again!" But that's not what happened. Instead, I collapsed on my friend Sue's sofa with a box of tissues and didn't move much for quite a while. As I lay there, my predicament slowly came into focus. I—who had devoted much of my life to making sure I would be financially safe and secure both through work and marriage—had handed my husband that power and now found my economic stability vanished within a matter of weeks. Just like that, I'd fallen through my carefully crafted safety net.

In my stunned and prone state, something became very clear: I could no longer afford the murky and oblique relationship to money I had maintained for most of my adult life. I had to admit that I held a good deal of responsibility for my situation. It was the price I paid for not wanting to think about my financial state, and it explained how I, an independent woman with twenty-plus years of career behind her, had come to be splayed on a couch in San Francisco, watching as El Niño dumped buckets of water down the steep hills and the gray streets.

What is so troublesome about our relationship with money that we're so elusive or dishonest about it—to ourselves, to others? When it comes to money, many of us are completely contradictory, often evasive, and irritatingly indirect. We won't ask people about their incomes, yet we peg our social positions by where we *think* we stand comparatively. We disguise our appetites by manufacturing "needs." We never reveal how much money we make, or what we have in the bank. We defiantly spend when we know we shouldn't. We're reluctant (sometimes afraid) to negotiate for better salaries and find it humiliating to haggle over prices. We amaze our husbands, lovers, and friends with reports of the things we bought on sale that never ever were, and we routinely shave a few bucks off the cost of something as minor as a lipstick so we won't appear irresponsible.

Not only that; we've developed a whole moral vocabulary to describe our supposed disdain for money: greedy, miserly, moneygrubbing, gold-digging, dirt-poor, nouveau riche, stinking rich, well-off, well-to-do—the list goes on and on. But we can come up with only a few sympathetic descriptors: self-supporting, independent, generous…self-made and enterprising can cut both ways. These adjectives reflect our emotions about money: greed, envy, guilt, even shame. It turns out we feel that liking money is somewhat immoral.

We need money and resent the fact that we do. We want it, we like to spend it, and we know that just admitting that qualifies us as potentially superficial and materialistic people. We may condemn our wants as crass consumerism, yet we can be stopped dead in our tracks at the thought of losing our lifestyles. We regularly want more than we can afford, which leaves us in a semipermanent state of deprivation.

Buffeted by alternating currents, we either engage in debt-defying impulse spending or plunge our heads in the sand in an effort to drown out our financial anxieties.

We can deny that money matters to us as much as we want, but then how do we explain the degree to which we've endowed it with all sorts of superpowers that can transform our emotional states? We've granted it the authority to single-handedly make us feel safe and cared for. We twist ourselves into impossible shapes to please and stay attached to the people and institutions that dole it out. Put it this way: If we behaved at work, with our friends, or with our husbands as indirectly, ambivalently, dishonestly, dependently as we do with money—we would immediately go into psychotherapy.

When it comes to our concerns about cash, we live in a land caught between our fears and our appetites. What do we do with this money anxiety? For many of us, our response has been a kind of voluntary blindness. We don't mind making money. We don't mind being in charge of our financial destinies. We just don't want to have to *think* about it too much.

This twisted relationship—and the guilt, embarrassment, reluctance, and avoidance that are involved—can have some serious consequences. In the course of my research, I heard stories from women like Amanda, a nurse who felt so badly about leaving her ten-year marriage to her first husband (who would routinely loan her car, her clothes, her books, and her jewelry to others because, after all, he said, he paid for them, and so they were his to give) that she didn't ask for a dime. She had so much baggage around money, she said, that she didn't want to face the fight and put a price on her life with him. Rather than ask for alimony, she enlisted in the army to pay for her college education. Now, as a single mom with a set of young twins, she can be called into conflict at any minute. Or women like Nancy, a stay-at-home mom who entertained lavishly in a beautiful home that she renovated or redecorated every five years but who hasn't had sex with her husband in ten.

Although I met some women who were truly direct about and in control of their finances, most of the rest of us clearly aren't. More women will file for bankruptcy this year than will graduate from college, suffer a heart attack, or be diagnosed with cancer. More than half of all retired women live in poverty. A family with children is 75 percent more likely to be late paying its credit card bills, and according to the work done by Harvard's Elizabeth Warren and Amelia Warren Tyagi, the single biggest predictor that a woman will end up in financial collapse is the birth of a child.

So with all this at stake, why is that so many of us don't just "get over it"— as my friend Carole suggested to me one morning over coffee—and deal with our money issues? Why do perfectly brilliant and sensible women admit that their eyes glaze over when individual household budgets and broader financial matters are discussed? Why the drive to spend beyond our means, why the willed insecurity about investing? Why the inability to ask to be paid what a job is worth? Why do we want to earn money and still be "taken care of" by someone else?

Of course, there are women who are very comfortable with money, who happily and intelligently handle not only their own finances but also those of their families and their corporations. They either had never experienced or had moved beyond an emotional relationship with money. When I began my inquiries, I had assumed these would be the younger women, those who had grown up in an age of post-feminist fiscal equality. And there were some who fell into that group. But for the most part, it was maturity and experience that created harmony and acceptance, not time and place of birth. The women I found who had the healthiest relationships possessed an honesty and a clarity about what money could and couldn't do for their lives. They'd managed to unpack their emotions from their finances, and they took care of themselves with confidence. They were able to bring the same understanding to money that they had brought to issues with their families, their weight, their work, and even their love lives. Their stories inspired me, but, I admit that at first I felt a little out of my league. Yet by the end of my investigation, I began to grasp a little bit of their peace of mind.

I've been rich, and I've also been poor (and as Sophie Tucker famously quipped, "Rich is better"), and I've inhabited most points along the middle-class spectrum. I've married a wealthy man and one a bit more "fiscally challenged." I've enjoyed years of financial stability, a few of downright largesse, and some that were a little too much on the rocky side for my taste. Now, as I approach my middle-aged years, just when I thought I'd have a modicum of security, I still live paycheck to paycheck, wondering if I've saved enough to support myself in my old age. I'm a woman, like the women in this book, who has spent a lot of time thinking about what makes us truly independent emotionally, spiritually, physically, and yet, fiscally.

So I'm putting my experiences down on paper with the full knowledge that I'm one of the most fortunate women in the world. I've enjoyed the benefits of a great education, supportive family, and excellent career opportunities. Make no mistake; I consider my financial fears a privilege. I am acutely aware that the tyranny of choice is not even a pale shadow in the face of the tyranny of need. And I feel guilty, like so many women I have spoken with, that I have so much and still feel so anxious.

Look through dictionaries, thesauruses, and web resources to add to Perle's "moral vocabulary to describe our supposed disdain for money." What words besides "self-supporting, independent, [and] generous," seem to sympathetically describe wealth? How can you characterize the other words we use to describe money and the people who have it?

Analyze the details that Perle chooses to illustrate her own relationship to money. How do the details that she shares represent (or evoke) a kind of money anxiety that transcends a simple bottom-line economics? In other words, how is money a part of who we are—what we want, how we think of ourselves, the ways we plan our futures? How does the narrative style of the essay—opposed, for instance, to an impersonal collection of statistics and interviews—affect the way Perle approaches this question.

Perle's opening biographical account of her marriage breaking up in Singapore, and the research that her story compels her to do, examine money as a complicated entity for women in particular. What would you think if the genders in the opening narrative were reversed: a husband who has moved for his wife's work being sent home with only $1500 to his name? In your group, discuss whether you think women have a different relationship to money than men do. Reflect on the men and women you observed growing up—parents, grandparents, family friends. Who controlled the money? Who, if anyone, seemed to have a more honest or comfortable relationship to it? In your group's experience, does the current generation of young adults have different attitudes toward gender and money than their parents' generation?

Jared Bernstein is a writer and economist, and until recently Chief Economic Advisor to Vice President Joe Biden. Currently, he is a senior fellow at the Center on Budget and Policy Priorities. This article is taken from his 2008 book Crunch: Why Do I Feel So Squeezed? (And Other Economic Mysteries). *He attempts, in layman terms, to explain common thought in economics: from teacher's pay to income distribution.*

WHY DO TEACHERS MAKE SO LITTLE?

BY JARED BERNSTEIN

Why do teachers make so little compared with stock traders? Aren't the teachers entrusted with greater responsibilities?

Economists have an answer to this that's as simple as it is unsatisfying: People are paid what they're worth. That is, they are paid according to the value they add to the economy.

It's your classic, pristine economic assumption: If, by definition, you're paid according to your "value added," you cannot, by definition, be under- or overpaid. If you think you're earning too little, then you must be placing an inflated value on your self-worth. Your economic self-esteem is too high.

How do I know this is wrong? Oh, come on…can't I just assert it? Does anyone really believe that people are paid their precise worth? How come other people get to make bogus assumptions and I've gotta prove everything?!

(Sorry—excuse the rant. We're back live.)

Contradictions abound, in fact. People doing a job in high-end firms get paid more than those doing the same job in low-end ones, like janitors at Goldman Sachs versus those at the dockside warehouse. Union workers make more than nonunion workers doing the same job. Even when we control for all the relevant differences (experience, occupation, education), women and minorities earn less than white men (and 75 percent of public school teachers are women). Most recently, earnings have stagnated—the real weekly earnings of the typical (median) worker were down slightly between 2000 and 2006.

Yet the economy's productivity rose 17 percent. There is simply, absolutely, unequivocally no way that people were being paid commensurate with their contributions to the economy over those years.

Not that there's no relationship between value added and earnings, but a million other factors come into play. Let's examine a few regarding the question posed above.

First, the motivation behind this question is usually something like: "Teachers are educating our future citizens and workforce, while stock traders are making bets that Ukrainian oil futures will fall relative to Bulgarian wheat prices. Shouldn't society value the former more than the latter?"

Well, part of what determines your pay in occupations like law, finance, and real estate, for example, is the money you bring in through the door. Successful traders bring in a lot; successful teachers don't bring in any. So, part of the answer is that traders and lawyers and such folks are literally working with the coin of the realm. Valuing teachers' work, which is really more like valuing an investment, takes a little more thought.

How, in fact, should we evaluate teachers' "output"? The rage nowadays is to hold teachers and schools accountable for test scores. While this sounds like a reasonable metric, there are countless factors that affect a student's ability to learn, and some of the most important ones are at work outside the realm of education and inside the realm of family.

And even if we could have faith in such output measures and they led us to believe we should pay teachers more, where would that lead us? Right to the taxpayer.

Herein lies the other rub. Teachers, at least the majority of the K-12 ones who work in the public sector, get paid through taxes, mostly local ones. And that can be a terribly tough wedge between what you get and what you're worth. Communities are constantly squabbling over this issue, and if you've ever been to a town meeting, you know how contentious this gets. Those asking taxpayers to pony up more bucks for teacher pay can't point to a new library, a ball field, or another such structure. They've got to make the case that this is the right investment.

Teachers' unions get villainized, and you can find examples where lousy teachers were unduly protected by the union. But all of the above discussion tells you why you really need unions here: Without them, the teachers would have little bargaining clout against those who would devalue their work. To the contrary, let us now forget principle #1 regarding the role of power in determining economic outcomes. We should thank the unions for trying to keep teachers' pay high enough to attract decent people to the job.

And, in fact, in terms of compensation, the unions aren't as successful as their detractors make them out to be. Careful research shows that we underpay teachers. Even accounting for the fact that most of them work fewer hours per year than comparably skilled professionals (that is, controlled for education, age, and other relevant characteristics), when we compare their pay with that of other such workers, they earn less than they should.

Use the web, public databases, job ads in newspapers, or even phone calls to local businesses, to explore salaries in your area. What are starting salaries for elementary school teachers where you live? What are average salaries across all ranges of experience? What are the starting and average salaries for high school teachers? For instructors at your college? Compare these numbers to the wages for entry-level work in other occupations that require a college degree, and then to occupations that don't. How does work seem to be valued: by skill, knowledge, demand, status, measureable output?

The author claims that "part of what determines your pay in occupations like law, finance, and real estate... is the money you bring in through the door," but teachers "don't bring in any" (page 42). He offers test scores as one of the most easily identifiable measures of teachers' work "output." What else, though, might count as "output," or other criteria on which teachers' work should be measured?

Money

Robert M. Franklin, Jr. is president of Morehouse College and a scholar in ethics, religions, and politics. Prior to his current position, he served on the faculties at Harvard, University of Chicago, and Emory. He is the author of a number of books including Another Day's Journey: Black Churches Confronting the American Crisis and Crisis in the Village: Restoring Hope in African American Communities, from which Sojourner's magazine excerpted "The Gospel of Bling."

THE GOSPEL OF BLING

By Robert M. Franklin, Jr.

I am convinced that the single threat to the historical legacy and core values of the contemporary black church tradition is posed by what is known as the "prosperity gospel" movement. That movement, however, is only symptomatic of a larger mission crisis or "mission drift" that has placed the black church in the posture of assimilating into a culture that is hostile to people living on the margins of society, such as people living in poverty, people living with AIDS, homosexuals, and immigrants.

This is not a new challenge. Christians have grappled with their relationship to material goods and opportunities in this world since the first century. But in our era something new and different has emerged. Today, prominent, influential, and attractive preachers and representatives of the church now are advocates for prosperity. Perhaps this could only occur at a time and in a place where two conditions exist. First, Christianity is the dominant faith tradition; second, the nation permits and rewards extraordinary inequalities of wealth and power.

The gospel of assimilation provides sacred sanction for personal greed, obsessive materialism, and unchecked narcissism. That distorted gospel dares not risk a critique of the culture and systems that thrive in the presence of a morally anemic church. This is more than a concern about the encroachment of the prosperity gospel movement that receives so much negative attention. Rather, this is a more thorough and comprehensive distortion of the religion of Jesus.

To be a successful (different from faithful) pastor in today's world is to confront the ever-present temptation to sell one's soul, compromising one's vocation and ethical responsibilities, in exchange for or access to wealth. One Houston-based minister observed that when the church gets a mortgage, "poor people" become just another church program. Poor people were central to Jesus's own self-definition, but they are often relegated to one of many service programs of today's corporate church, simply another item on the services menu.

The tragedy is that one-fourth of the black community lives in poverty while many clergy and churches are distracted and seduced by the lure of material wealth. When churches devote more time to building their local kingdoms and less time to nurturing and uplifting poor people, they are struggling with a mission crisis.

A PROSPERITY FIELD TRIP

One Sunday, I visited the church of my Atlanta neighbor, the Rev. Creflo Dollar. I had heard about the burgeoning ministry of the World Changers Church and felt I should see for myself.

I found a parking space three blocks from the sanctuary. The hike to the sanctuary was so far that I momentarily forgot where I was headed and began to window shop the stores en route to the church, perhaps unconsciously getting into prosperity mode. I finally arrived and entered the enormous domed sanctuary, taking a seat near the front. Everything was neat and comfortable. The blue carpet and plush pew covers were welcoming. The huge rotating globe and other props on stage subtly reminded one that what happens here is intended for a global television audience.

After the choir sang, Rev. Dollar entered the sanctuary dressed in a business power suit and took his seat. Most black preachers begin their sermons in a conversational way. They acknowledge the presence of special guests and familiar faces and invite people to relax and laugh before they begin the journey toward an encounter with the holy. But this was a bit different, perhaps because the stage lights and television cameras were operating. Dispensing with all of the "old school" black church conventions, he went right to the text for the day.

The first 15 minutes of his message were encouraging and impressive. I heard evidence of a critical thinker who had done his homework and given careful attention to various scholarly sources for the selected biblical text. Then, out of nowhere, he began to testify about a friend who had recently given him a second Rolls Royce. He continued, "Now, that's not the Rolls that you all gave me years ago. See, so don't get mad. This was a gift from a friend." I wonder if anyone else wondered, "Why does he need one Rolls Royce? But, two?"

More amazing was that the congregation seemed to affirm this testimony of personal indulgence and excess. No one seemed to have the power to hold the preacher accountable for exceeding his proper allowance as a representative of Jesus. I do not know Rev. Dollar personally and I will reserve judgment about his motives and character, but it appears he has followed the script for how a successful and affluent corporate executive behaves. He does not seem to have entertained the possibility of rewriting that script and offering to other ministers and followers a new paradigm of socially responsible affluence.

If most black preachers—and other preachers for that matter—are preoccupied with pursuing the "bling-bling" life of conspicuous consumption, then poor people are in big trouble, because it indicates that the hearts of their chief advocates are "drunk with the wine of the world," to use James Weldon Johnson's phrase, and incapable of speaking truth to power.

Given the distorting influence of the prosperity movement on authentic Christianity, I should say more about the phenomenon.

We should distinguish between three realities: First, the "gospel of prosperity." Second, the "prosperity gospel." And third, radical Christian stewardship that may include the ownership of material goods.

The gospel of prosperity: "Greed is good." The "gospel of prosperity" refers to the cultural ideology that suggests that the accumulation of material possessions, wealth, and prosperity are morally neutral goods that are necessary for human happiness. I characterize it as an ideology rather than merely an idea because it functions like a powerful, unconscious force that does not revise its position in the face of counterevidence. For instance, its advocates would not admit that possessing material goods in excess may actually induce unhappiness. As an ideology, its believers insist upon its correctness, deny the legitimacy of other perspectives, and pursue wealth without concern for long-term consequences. Prosperity becomes an intrinsic good and an end in itself.

Most examples of this vulgar form of material worship do not pretend to be religious, certainly not Christian. Rather, they are elements of what might be called America's largest quasi-religious tradition, namely the religion of capitalism. The gospel of prosperity has been a guiding ideology or myth embodied in the Horatio Alger story (among others), where people acquire wealth through the heroic exercise of risk-taking, ingenuity, high energy, inordinate self-confidence, and tireless effort. That's the gospel of prosperity that underwrites American capitalism. The gospel of prosperity is a competitor to authentic Christianity (and other faith traditions) and ruthlessly seeks to establish its preeminence in the culture.

The prosperity gospel of the spiritual entrepreneurs. The "prosperity gospel" asserts that Christian faith is an investment that yields material abundance. Rev. Dollar fits in this category, along with scores of other televangelists who live and instruct others on how to "think and grow rich." Wealth is outward proof of an inner grace and righteousness. Salvation is both spiritual and material. And although the "prosperity gospel" may not be as vulgar an expression of greed as the "'gospel of prosperity," both are corrosive and threatening to American churches, which are constantly tempted to focus on their own institutional well-being at the expense of serving the vulnerable.

The prosperity gospel may be even more insidious and dangerous because it subverts particular elements of the Jesus story and of classical biblical Christianity in order to instill a new attitude toward capitalism and riches. It often deliberately suppresses, ignores, and/or deletes language about radical sacrifice for the sake of God's kingdom. In other words, it excludes a core message of the Jesus story, namely that which is symbolized by the cross. That symbol is an enemy to the underlying confidence people invest in material prosperity at the expense of trusting God. "Cross talk" insists that believers share their material prosperity rather than hoard it. At times the call to share wealth may be so radical that a person is compelled to give it all away in order to serve and please God.

I refer to the clergy who operate from this orientation as "spiritual entrepreneurs" who know how to produce, package, market, and distribute user-friendly spirituality for the masses. The spiritual product lines they market rarely make stringent ethical demands upon their listeners. Instead, they proffer a gospel of health, wealth, and success designed to help others become more affluent. When these leaders serve as pastors of congregations, they function like "entrepreneurial ecclesiastical executives" at the helm of corporate organizations. Such congregations and leaders may be changing who they are and are called to be, distorting the meaning of church as a community of holy awareness, care, interdependence, sharing, moral deliberation, and action.

PROPHETIC STEWARDSHIP

A third view of faith and money is "prophetic stewardship." I use the word prophetic to emphasize that this model represents something of a negative judgment on its alternatives, the secular gospel of prosperity and the pseudo-religious prosperity gospel. It seeks to displace them with a more radical version of stewardship and shared prosperity. Here it is understood that the Christian gospel includes many goods—spiritual, social, psychological, physical, and material. But none of them, apart from the spiritual good of salvation, is promised without qualification. Again, the cross and a disciple's faithful embrace of it may require one to practice what theologian Jacquelyn Grant has called an "ethic of renunciation," in which we may have to sacrifice physical well-being, psychological comfort, social support, and material goods for the sake of saving our souls. Is this the meaning of Matthew 6:33, "But, seek ye first the kingdom of God and his righteousness and all these things shall be added to you"?

Prophetic stewardship invites reflection upon the meaning of the values found in passages such as Matthew 6:19-20. There, Jesus engages in "cross talk" as he declares "do not store up for yourselves treasures on earth where moth and rust destroy and where thieves break in and steal, but store up for yourselves treasures in heaven." Acts 2:44-45 indicates that "All the believers were together and had everything in common; selling their possessions and goods, they gave to anyone as he had need." When people had a life-changing encounter with Jesus, it also reshaped their attitude toward their possessions.

Prophetic stewardship is the most adequate and authentic expression of a Christian orientation to money. Consequently, Christians should aspire to understand, accept, and practice prophetic stewardship. Such stewardship both encourages Christians to live in a simple but comfortable manner (leaving a small footprint on the earth) and publicly works to change the culture's prevailing habits of greed. This public move is what makes it prophetic. That is, prosperity per se should never become a prominent theme or mark of the faithful Christian life. It should never compete with the cross for center stage. Material acquisition should always be incidental to one's vocation and one must always be prepared to make radical sacrifices for the sake of one's soul and/or the good of the reign of God.

Against the background of the prosperity gospel movement and the seductions of spiritual leaders is the more chilling report that many churches located in high poverty neighborhoods are not responding to local needs effectively. Rev. Drew Smith, a senior fellow at the Leadership Center of Morehouse College, undertook research in four cities on the relationship between churches and low-income residents. His 2003 report, "Beyond the Boundaries: Low-Income Residents, Faith-Based Organizations and Neighborhood Coalition Building," states the following conclusions:

Two-thirds of the housing complex residents surveyed report having little or no contact with faith-based organizations in the previous year; many congregations report having programs of potential value to neighborhood residents but indicate that church members take advantage of these programs more frequently than non-members; and roughly two-thirds of the congregations report that most of their members live more than one mile from their place of worship.

Smith and others underscore the social isolation of low-income, urban residents from the jobs, social services, and poverty-alleviating networks in their metro areas. And he points to the potential of churches to bridge that distance and help to connect people and their communities.

I hope that the disconnect between churches and their local neighborhoods will become an issue that evokes conversation about how congregations that do little for local residents can revise their ministries to serve them more effectively. And I hope that the same community that criticizes inactive churches will acknowledge and reward those who are active and faithful to their mission.

Why are churches so susceptible to misreading or misplacing their moral compasses? The work that Jesus left for the church is clearly set forth in the New Testament, and the people he wanted us to assist and empower are clearly identified. Moreover, Jesus provided the means for doing effective ministry before he departed. So what's the problem? I would submit that leadership, its quality, performance, and education, are essential.

The irony is that many black preachers stylistically present themselves to the world as large, powerful, and accomplished individuals. How many of today's denominational leaders, local pastors, or founders of the new megachurches have risked their access to important people or revenue streams in order to achieve goals in the arena of social justice, such as dismantling penalties against the working poor, expanding health-care coverage, or dramatically improving the well-being of children?

We must invite and challenge leaders to do the right things, to do them more effectively, and in a collaborative manner. Further, we should reward institutions and leaders that meet our expectations and ignore those who are unresponsive or deliberately clueless. Moreover, we should actively isolate, stigmatize, and discourage those who are harmful to our communities. This must never be done in a mean-spirited way, but we must not permit leaders who exploit people to think that the community approves of such poor stewardship. The community deserves prophetic stewards.

Franklin's article contrasts two paradigms: what he defines as "prosperity gospel," and what he refers to as the "black church tradition," but from the beginning, with language of "threat" and "crisis," his opinion on their relative merits is clear. Do some research to come up with your own working definitions and assess the qualities of these positions. First, look around on the internet for organizations that implicitly or explicitly embody these ideologies; then, critically examine their websites. What do they claim to believe? On what do they base their claims? Is Franklin's critique of prosperity gospel theology valid? Is his view of historically black churches idealized? How do the sites themselves differ in visual style? Rhetoric? Intended audiences?

The New Testament declares that the "love of money is the root of all kinds of evil" (1 Timothy 6:10). Though he doesn't quote this verse, Franklin states his own point bluntly: "prophetic stewardship is the most adequate and authentic expression of a Christian orientation to money" (page 49). Do you agree? Are there factors that Franklin seems not to consider? How would this philosophy function on a day-to-day basis? Would a Christian have to give up all material comforts to satisfy Franklin's definition? How is your personal ideological orientation—faith system or ethical code—compatible with your own attitude toward wealth?

Imagine that you've suddenly come into a lot of (honestly gained) money—you've invented a product that's become phenomenally successful, started a website that's rocketed in popularity, starred in a video gone viral that has brought about celebrity beyond your wildest dreams. What would you do with all that money? How would your spending decisions reflect your core values? What, if any, social or political ramifications would your decisions have? Is that important? Why or why not?

Jim Picht is a linguist and economics professor at the Louisiana Scholar's College at Northwestern State University. His column, "Stimulus That!" appears in the Communities section of the Washington Times online. In "Burning Down the House" Picht discusses the arguments surrounding the September 2010 fire in which the local fire department did nothing to prevent a man's house from burning because he hadn't paid his fire district fee.

BURNING DOWN THE HOUSE

BY JIM PICHT

By now everyone who reads or watches the news has heard about Gene Cranick, the man whose house near South Fulton, Tennessee, burned down while firefighters stood by watching. The opinions have flown thicker than smoke, Ayn Rand conservatives opining "serves him right, the fool, he should have paid the fire protection fee," bleeding heart liberals countering, "fire protection is as much a right as emergency medical care, and what kind of crummy society lets a man's house burn down?" Keith Olbermann goes further, arguing that this sad story is a parable for what America will be if we don't defeat the Tea Party. The left seems incapable of discussing the fire without emphasizing that the government of South Fulton is Republican.

Before we start opining, it's always good to marshal a few facts: Fact One: Firefighting isn't free. If it isn't paid for, it won't be there. It can be paid for either by taxes or by fees, and in either case its provision can be universal, but costs will be distributed in very different ways.

Fact Two: If people are allowed to pay for the services of the fire department only after they receive them, those services will be extremely expensive. If a community experiences a hundred house fires in a year, the hundred families involved will end up paying the entire cost of firefighters' salaries, equipment, fire-station expenses and so on for the year. For many, it would be cheaper just to let the house burn down.

Fact Three: A public good is a good that must be provided to all if it's provided to any in a society. Consumption isn't rivalrous or excludable. By that narrow definition, fire departments don't provide a public good. In dense urban settings we might insist that they exclude no one (one burning house will ignite others in the neighborhood), but in rural settings there's no immediate danger to my house if my neighbor's burns.

Fact Four: While Cranick didn't pay his $75 fee for fire protection (and he didn't pay it last year, either), he apparently paid his insurance premiums and, as he reported to Olbermann, the insurance company is "on top of it."

"Aha!" the liberals say, "You're on the side of Glenn Beck and Ayn Rand!" In fact, no. Rand was an interesting thinker with some perceptive insights on law and economics, but I'd hate to live in a society that adhered to her precepts. "Bleeding heart," my conservative readers mutter. Not at all. Cranick and his family deserved to pay a stiff penalty for their failure to pay for fire protection. I just don't think that society is well-served by making that penalty their entire house and all their possessions.

Standard economic thinking says that if the cost of putting out a house fire in South Fulton is less than the value of the property saved, the fire should be put out. The cost of firefighting services can be taken from the property owner afterwards. If the value of the property is less, the house should burn. What if there are people inside? We can stipulate that the value of human life exceeds the cost of putting out the typical house fire and put the fire out. It's bad for society to simply let resources burn if they can be saved at lower resource cost.

It's also bad for society to remove incentives to people to take responsibility for their property and their decisions. The Cranick's shouldn't have been allowed just to pay the $75 after the fact, as some have argued. If you let people buy insurance only after they get sick, there will be no insurance. They'll end up having to pay the full cost of medical services. The services should be provided, but if we're going to dispense with insurance (the sure outcome if non-payers are covered by it), then we should expect to pay for our full share of that MRI scanner or that fire engine and the people who make them work rather than spreading the costs with the risk.

I prefer to pay for my fire protection through taxes. So, it seems, does Olbermann. That's not an argument against other arrangements, like that in South Fulton, but I do argue that the South Fulton model needs revision. It's indecent to stand by and watch a family's house burn, and I don't want people who provide emergency services to be hardened into indecency. I don't think that decency should be mandatory to anyone who lives in our society, but it should be encouraged. So should responsibility, which is why we should take however much salvaged property we need to from non-paying fire victims to ensure that fire departments continue to operate and that no one free ride on that service.

People like Rand and Beck have sound minds and too little heart. People like Olbermann are all passionate heart and underused brain cells. Genuine morality and compassion require that we balance mind and heart, not something we do in our super-heated political climate. Good public policy often requires "tough love," but tough love is only good so long as we ignore neither necessary toughness nor genuine love. Otherwise we're left with mewling and ineffectual compassion or brutal self-interest.

Using newspapers, news magazines, and news and opinion websites, learn all you can about the Cranick fire. Skim not only for factual information but for personal reactions, everywhere from editorials like Picht's to message board conversations beneath internet news and opinion pieces online. What details seem important to you? Does Picht include all the most significant aspects of the situation, in your opinion? What other things might be relevant, whether you have found the information or not?

Consider Picht's analysis of the rhetoric on the two sides of this debate. Is he right to characterize the left as all heart and the right as all brain? Can you imagine logical arguments for a fire department's deciding to put out Cranick's fire, or emotion-based arguments against?

What are the implications of this debate? In your small group, brainstorm a list of public services that, like fire service in rural Louisiana, could theoretically become fee-based or private rather than the "public good" that we might otherwise expect. For which of these would the decision of the Natchitoches firefighters set an appropriate precedent? For which does it seem inappropriate?

Bill Watterson began his career as a political cartoonist for the Cincinnati Post and as a commercial artist. The Calvin & Hobbes strip was first published in 1985, and Watterson ended its run in 1995. Inspired by Peanuts, Pogo, and Krazy Kat, Calvin & Hobbes features a young boy and his stuffed toy tiger, Hobbes, who comes alive when Calvin and Hobbes are alone. Watterson uses these two characters to critique society and culture. Watterson was highly critical of merchandising Calvin & Hobbes and allowed almost no products, save book collections, to be made. Any products bearing their likeness are almost undoubtedly counterfeit.

CALVIN & HOBBES
MONEY, POWER, OR FAME

BY BILL WATTERSON

Do you agree with Calvin's assertion in the second panel of the strip? Why or why not? What do you think Hobbes's reservations are?

Write a journal entry or blog post in which you reflect on what you think the secret to happiness is. How does money relate to your ideas?

Pulitzer Prize winner George Will's syndicated newspaper columns are widely read across the U.S., and he is a founding member of the panel on ABC's This Week with Christiane Amanpour. "A Lexus in Every Garage" is a response to the leaked Citigroup report on plutonomy (a term the report writers coined to mean economic growth made and used by the wealthiest in a society). In effect, the report writers discuss their research on investments in products and services aimed at the wealthy, asserting that those investments will continue to do well given conditions conducive to plutonomy: capitalist government, technology, globalization, patent protection, and rule of law.

A LEXUS IN EVERY GARAGE

By George F. Will

Enough, already, with compassion for society's middle and lower orders. There currently is a sympathy deficit regarding the very rich. Or so the rich might argue because they bear the heavy burden of spending enough to keep today's plutonomy humming.

Furthermore, they are getting diminishing psychological returns on their spending now that luxury brands are becoming democratized. When there are 379 Louis Vuitton and 227 Gucci stores, who cares?

Citigroup's Ajay Kapur applies the term "plutonomy" to, primarily, the United States, although Britain, Canada and Australia also qualify. He notes that America's richest 1 percent of households own more than half the nation's stocks and control more wealth ($16 trillion) than the bottom 90 percent. When the richest 20 percent account for almost 60 percent of consumption, you see why rising oil prices have had so little effect on consumption.

Kapur's theory is that "wealth waves" develop in epochs characterized by, among other things, disruptive technology-driven productivity gains and creative financial innovations that "involve great complexity exploited best by the rich and educated of the time." For the canny, daring and inventive, these are the best of times—and vast rewards to such people might serve the rapid propulsion of society to greater wealth.

But it is increasingly expensive to be rich. The Forbes CLEW index (the Cost of Living Extremely Well)—yes, there is such a thing—has been rising much faster than the banal CPI (consumer price index). At the end of 2006, there were 9.5 million millionaires worldwide, which helps to explain the boom in the "bling indexes"—stocks such as Christian Dior and Richemont (Cartier and Chloe, among other brands), which are up 247 percent and 337 percent respectively since 2002, according to Fortune magazine. Citicorp's "plutonomy basket" of stocks (Sotheby's, Bulgari, Hermes, etc.) has generated an annualized return of 17.8 percent since 1985.

This is the outer symptom of a fascinating psychological phenomenon: Envy increases while—and perhaps even faster than—wealth does. When affluence in the material economy guarantees that a large majority can take for granted things that a few generations ago were luxuries for a small minority (a nice home, nice vacations, a second home, college education, comfortable retirement), the "positional economy" becomes more important.

Positional goods and services are *inherently* minority enjoyments. These are enjoyments—"elite" education, "exclusive" vacations or properties—available only to persons with sufficient wealth to pursue the satisfaction of "positional competition." Time was, certain clothes, luggage, wristwatches, handbags, automobiles, etc. sufficed. But with so much money sloshing around the world, too many people can purchase them. Too many, in the sense that the value of acquiring a "positional good" is linked to the fact that all but a few people cannot acquire it.

That used to be guaranteed because supplies of many positional goods were inelastic—they were made by a small class of European craftsmen. But when they are mass-produced in developing nations, they cannot long remain such goods. When 40 percent of all Japanese—and, Fortune reports, 94.3 percent of Japanese women in their 20s—own a Louis Vuitton item, its positional value vanishes.

James Twitchell, University of Florida professor of English and advertising, writing in the *Wilson Quarterly*, says this "lux populi" is "the Twinkiefication of deluxe." Now that Ralph Lauren is selling house paint, can Polo radial tires be far behind? When a yacht manufacturer advertises a $20 million craft—in a newspaper, for Pete's sake; the *Financial Times*, but still—cachet is a casualty.

As Adam Smith wrote in *The Wealth of Nations*, for most rich people "the chief enjoyment of riches consists in the parade of riches, which in their eye is never so complete as when they appear to possess those decisive marks of opulence which nobody can possess but themselves." Hennessy understands the logic of trophy assets: It is selling a limited batch of 100 bottles of cognac for $200,000 a bottle.

There is some good news lurking amid the vulgarity. Americans' saving habits are better than they seem because the very rich, consuming more than their current earnings, have a *negative* savings rate.

Furthermore, because the merely affluent are diminishing the ability of the very rich to derive pleasure from positional goods, philanthropy might become the final form of positional competition. Perhaps that is why so many colleges and universities (more than 20, according to Twitchell) are currently conducting multi *billion*-dollar pledge campaigns. When rising consumption of luxuries produces declining enjoyment of vast wealth, giving it away might be the best revenge.

What do you own that sets you apart from others? Does it bear class markers (that is, does it advertise that you are from a specific economic class (a Coach bag, a Mercedes, an Armani suit)?

Will notes that affluence has been on the rise over the last few decades and that people now have luxuries they didn't have before. This statement seems to fly in the face of economic data provided in the Wolff piece (page 69). Research what the average family of the 1920s, 1950s, and 1990s had. Interview your parents, grandparents, and great grandparents to test Will's assertion.

Since 2008, Bethany McLean has been a contributing editor for Vanity Fair magazine. Working at Fortune magazine in March 2001, McLean wrote an article questioning the value of the energy-trading and services company Enron. By December, Enron had filed for bankruptcy, and in subsequent years Jeffrey Skilling, Ken Rice, and Kenneth Lay among others were convicted of a host of felonies related to Enron's business and accounting practices. Peter Elkind is an editor at large for Fortune magazine. Besides writing about Enron, he has also written about Eliot Spitzer, former crusading prosecutor and governor of New York as well as Genene Jones, a nurse in the "Texas baby murders." Elkind has also written for The New York Times Magazine and The Washington Post.

excerpt from

THE SMARTEST GUYS IN THE ROOM

BY BETHANY MCLEAN AND PETER ELKIND

During his years running ECT, Skilling had led small groups of Enron executives and customers (all male, of course) on daredevil expeditions to the Australian outback; to Baja, Mexico; and to the glaciers of Patagonia. His goal, Ken Rice said later, was to find an adventure "where someone could actually get killed."

The Baja trip—a 1,200-mile road race in Jeeps and on dirt bikes—was particularly hairy. Only three members of the group (including Rice and Skilling) finished the entire course. Rice put a tooth through his lip when he slid off his bike. Another man barely escaped death when his 4X4 Jeep flipped end over end. A third broke several ribs after wiping out on his motorcycle; the first one on the scene was Andy Fastow, who promptly tumbled off an embankment and landed on a cactus. Others arrived to find the injured rider plucking cactus spines from Fastow's behind. The journey ended at a huge rented mansion in Cabo San Lucas called the Villa Golden Dome, where a chef had prepared a gourmet meal and a team of masseuses awaited the weary executives. Everyone was flown back to Houston on a chartered jet, and photo albums showcasing the expedition's highlights were later handed out. These trips entered Enron lore, serving as symbols of the company's macho, risk-taking culture.

For those at the top of Enron, excess was a part of daily life. Enron had a fleet of corporate jets, limousines on constant call, and even its own concierge, who would pick up busy employees' dry cleaning, water houseplants, and shop for anniversary presents. At bonus time, there was a rush on Houston's luxury car dealerships; flashy wheels (Porsches were a particular favorite) were de rigueur for top earners. Many built new homes and bought vacation properties or ranches. After living modestly for several years following his divorce, Skilling began construction on an 8,000-square-foot Mediterranean villa in River Oaks, full of modernist touches and with black-and-white décor. In Enron's work-hard, play-hard culture, the scent of sex was unmistakable; affairs flourished inside the company.

"Money went to those guys' heads," says a longtime Enron executive. "I used to walk off the company plane after being picked up and being dropped off by limousine, and I'd have to remind myself I was a real human being. You start living that life long enough, if you don't have very strong morals, you lose it fast. Enron was the kind of company that could spoil you pretty well."

That phenomenon clearly affected Ken Rice, the Nebraska farm boy who had once yanked nails for spending money. In the years after the Sithe deal, Rice found himself a multimillionaire while still in his mid-30s. He became caught up in the Enron whirl. Rice was one of the ringleaders of the daredevil trips Skilling organized; he developed a fondness for fast cars and motorcycles. Rice also had a reputation as a womanizer, and in 1996, while still married to his college sweetheart, he fell into Enron's most celebrated affair. The relationship became widely known because of the high-profile participants and because it lasted for three years.

Rice's mistress was Amanda Martin, who had worked at Enron since late 1991. A slim, stylish woman who had been raised on her family's sugar plantation in Zimbabwe, Martin had trained as a lawyer and come to ECT from Vinson & Elkins, the giant Houston law firm with close ties to the company. After starting out as an in-house lawyer, she ran a new group managing Enron's power plants worldwide for more than a year, then returned to ECT as a deal maker. In early 1995, she became ECT's first female managing director. In 1996, Martin was named president of North American origination and finance.

Martin's rapid rise was striking in ECT, with its lingering fondness for strip bars and its well-deserved reputation as a boys' club. One day in 1996, Martin received an interoffice envelope with an anonymous message: "Just thought you'd be interested to see this." Inside were computer printouts of the salary and bonus history of the male executives who had been promoted to managing director along with her. Everyone in the group had been promoted at the same time; all of them, including Martin, had consistently received a 1 performance ranking. Yet the printouts showed all the men were being paid $300,000 a year—Martin's base was $225,000—and had gotten bonuses that were at least $100,000 higher than hers for two consecutive years.

Martin immediately brought the documents to Skilling, who had often given her what he intended as a considerable compliment: "Amanda, you're one of the smartest women we have here." Now, insisting he knew nothing about the pay discrepancy, Skilling promised to look into it. Two weeks later, she received a check for $300,000. "Enron," says Martin, "was a hard place for a woman to work. It was like a boys' locker room."

At about the same time, though, Martin also made matters considerably more awkward for herself by beginning her relationship with Rice. The situation was messy. Both were married, with children (though Martin was separated from her husband). Rice was also Martin's boss. Not surprisingly, as the relationship became known, coworkers muttered that sleeping with the boss had accelerated her advance. One disgruntled ECT originator named Brian Barrington did more than mutter: he filed suit against the company and Rice, blaming the relationship for Rice's refusal to overturn Martin's decision to demote him. (The litigation aired some embarrassing discovery about Rice's sophomoric behavior before it was finally settled out of court.)

Skilling had first picked up complaints about the relationship a few months after it began. He confronted Rice, who denied that he was involved with Martin. But Skilling eventually realized that Rice had lied to him. Rice and Martin came clean and began appearing together in public, generating even more bitter complaints of favoritism. To deal with the complaints Skilling dispatched Martin to Rebecca Mark's new water company, Azurix. And Ken Rice? Nothing happened to him.

For his part, Skilling also began seeing someone from Enron, a woman named Rebecca Carter, a former Andersen accountant who worked on the trading floor as a risk manager. Skilling actually asked the board for permission to date her (after, according to several sources, their relationship had already begun).

Skilling also gave her a big promotion, naming her to the powerful post of corporate secretary, which put her in charge of organizing board meetings and taking the official minutes, among other duties. By the time she left Enron, her salary and bonus approached $600,000.

Which was yet another problem with Skilling's Enron. He still had his favorites, and they could still do no wrong. Skilling's handful of direct reports, noted Alkhayat, the COO's Egyptian-born aide, operated with his "blessed hand"; it was as if they'd been anointed by the leader as infallible and holy.

But they didn't consider Skilling infallible. It was a given, of course, that he was brilliant and that he could get to the essence of an issue faster than anybody. But once he felt he understood the strategy, he lost interest. Execution bored him. "Just do it!" he'd tell his subordinates with a dismissive wave of his hand. "Just get it done!" The details were irrelevant.

Many times, it wasn't even clear what Skilling wanted. He sometimes praised deals that had been carried out against his orders. He became enraptured with businesses he had initially dismissed. And he sometimes insisted he'd always opposed deals that he had actually embraced. When he gave specific directions, those unaccustomed to dealing with him sometimes made the mistake of following them too precisely. One longtime Skilling deputy says the boss's instructions at times required translation. "We'd understand where Jeff wanted to go and what he wanted to do. A lot of people who came over later would take him literally. They'd say: 'Jeff wants me to do this.' I'd say, 'Well, Jeff doesn't want you to do something *stupid!* He wants the end results. He doesn't know how to get there.'"

Consider the aspects of this description of corporate life at Enron that seem especially "masculine." What made this corporate environment one in which it was so difficult for women to succeed? Does there seem to be a relationship between money and a kind of "bad-boy" masculine identity elsewhere in our culture? How do you think this attitude affects gender equality in professional settings?

According to McLean, the "smartest guys in the room" at Enron traveled to exotic locations, drove some of the most expensive cars available, flew in private jets, and built 8,000 square foot homes. Are these executive expenditures portrayed in a positive, negative, or neutral light? Compare this excerpt to the Ariely piece (page 119) and discuss the relationship between money, power, and ethics. Is material excess necessarily bad? If so, is that an argument for capping salaries or otherwise limiting individual personal capital? Are there other reasons that these individuals should not have made as much money as they did?

MONEY

A professor of economics at New York University, Edward N. Wolff is the author of numerous books and articles including Does Education Really Help? Skill, Work, and Inequality *and* Downsizing in America: Reality, Causes, and Consequences *(with William J. Baumol and Alan Blinder). "Household Wealth Inequality in the United States" is chapter three from his 2002 book* Top Heavy: The Increasing of Wealth in America and What Can Be Done About It. *This piece looks at the numerical data behind the distribution of wealth in the United States.*

HOUSEHOLD WEALTH INEQUALITY IN THE UNITED STATES: PRESENT LEVELS AND HISTORICAL TRENDS

By Edward N. Wolff

Wealth inequality in the United States was at a seventy-year high in 1998 (the latest date available), with the top 1 percent of wealth holders controlling 38 percent of total household wealth. If we focus more narrowly, on financial wealth, the richest 1 percent of households owned 47 percent of the total. How did this come to pass? After the stock market crash of 1929, there ensued a gradual if somewhat erratic reduction in wealth inequality, which seems to have lasted until the late 1970s. Since then, inequality of wealth holdings, like that of income, has risen sharply (see Figure 1). If Social Security and other types of pension wealth ("augmented wealth") are included, the improvement between 1929 and 1979 appears greater, but the increase in inequality since 1980 is still sharply in evidence.

The rise in wealth inequality from 1983 to 1998 (a period for which there is comparable detailed household survey information) is particularly striking. The share of the top 1 percent of wealth holders rose by 5 percent. The wealth of the bottom 40 percent showed an absolute decline. Almost all the absolute gains in real wealth accrued to the top 20 percent of wealth holders.

Figure 1
Share of Wealth Owned By the Top 1 Percent of Households in the United States, 1922-1998

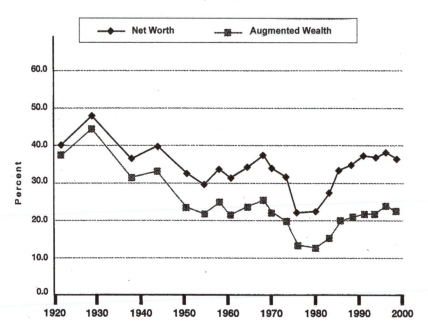

CHANGES IN AVERAGE WEALTH HOLDINGS

Look first at trends in real wealth over the period from 1962 to 1998 (all in 1998 dollars). As Figure 2 shows, average wealth grew at a respectable pace from 1962 to 1983 and even faster from 1983 to 1989. By 1989, the average wealth of households was $244,000 (in 1998 dollars), almost two-thirds higher than in 1962. From 1989 to 1998, wealth grew more slowly. In fact, mean marketable wealth grew only about half as fast between 1989 and 1998 as between 1983 and 1989 (1.2 percent per year versus 2.3 percent). Still, by 1998, average wealth had reached $270,000.

Figure 2
Annual Rate of Change in Real Income and Wealth 1962-1983, 1983-1989, and 1989-1998

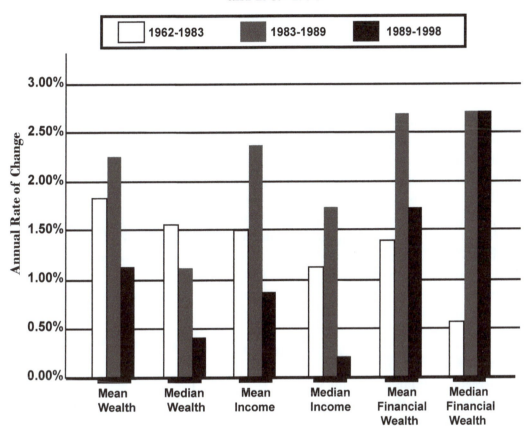

Source: 1962, from the Survey of Financial Characteristics of Consumers;
1983, 1989, and 1998, from the Survey of Consumer Finances

Average financial wealth grew faster than marketable wealth in the 1983-89 period (2.7 versus 2.3 percent per year), reflecting the increased importance of bank deposits, financial assets, equities, and small businesses in the overall household portfolio over this period. This reversed the relationship of the 1962-83 period, when financial wealth grew more slowly than marketable wealth (1.4 versus 1.8 percent per year). In the 1989-98 period, the gain in average financial wealth again outstripped net worth (1.7 versus 1.2 percent per year).

Average household income also grew faster in the 1983-89 period than in the 1962-83 period. Its annual growth accelerated from 1.5 percent to 2.4.

Whereas in the first of the two periods, average income grew more slowly than average wealth (a difference of 0.3 percentage points per year), in the latter it grew slightly faster (a difference of 0.1 percentage points per year). However, in the 1989-98 period, income growth plummeted to 0.9 percent per year (0.2 percentage points per year lower than wealth growth).

The robust growth of average wealth disguises some changes in the distribution of that wealth. This becomes clear after examination of median rather than mean wealth. Mean wealth is simply the average: total wealth divided by total number of households. If the wealth of only the top 20 percent of households increases (with nothing else changing), then mean wealth increases because total wealth increases. In contrast, the median of wealth distribution is defined as the level of wealth that divides the population of households into two equal-sized groups (those with more wealth than the median and those with less). Returning to the earlier example, if only the top quintile enjoys an increase in wealth, median wealth is unaffected even though mean wealth increases, because all additional wealth accrues to people well above the median income. The median tracks what is happening in the middle of wealth distribution. When trends in the mean deviate from trends in the median, this is a signal that gains and losses are unevenly distributed.

Figure 3
Percentage Shares of Total Wealth and Income of Percentile Groups in 1983, 1989, and 1998

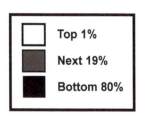

Top 1%
Next 19%
Bottom 80%

Source: 1980 and 1989 Survey
of Consumer Finances

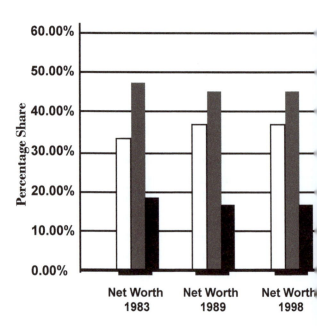

The trend in median household wealth in the United States gives a contrasting picture to the growth of mean wealth. Unlike mean marketable wealth, median marketable wealth grew faster in the 1962-83 period than in the 1983-89 period (1.6 percent versus 1.1 percent per year). Median wealth also grew much more slowly than mean wealth in the latter period (a difference of 0.8 percentage points per year). Overall, from 1983 to 1989, while mean wealth increased by 15 percent, median wealth grew by only 7 percent. The fact that mean wealth grew much faster than median wealth after 1983 implies that the bulk of the gains were concentrated at the top of the distribution—a finding that implies rising wealth inequality. The 1989-98 period was a repeat of the preceding one. While mean wealth grew 11 percent, median wealth increased by only 4 percent.

RISING WEALTH INEQUALITY IN THE 1980S

The rising level of wealth inequality between 1983 and 1989 is illustrated in Figure 3. The most telling finding is that the share of marketable net worth held by the top 1 percent, which had fallen 10 percentage points between 1945 and 1976, rose to 37 percent in 1989, compared with 34 percent in 1983. Meanwhile, the share of wealth held by the bottom 80 percent fell from 19 to 16 percent. Between 1989 and 1998, inequality continued to rise, though at a

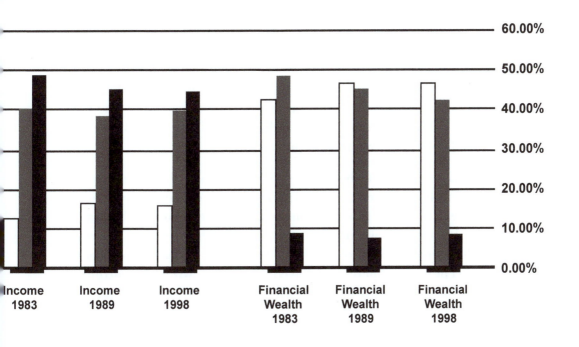

more moderate pace. The share of wealth held by the top 1 percent increased by another percentage point (to 38 percent), though the share of the bottom 80 percent stabilized.

These trends are mirrored in financial net worth, which is distributed even more unequally than total household wealth. In 1998, the top 1 percent of families as ranked by financial wealth owned 47 percent of the total (in contrast to 38 percent of total net worth). The top quintile accounted for 91 percent of total financial wealth, and the second quintile accounted for nearly all the remainder.

The concentration of financial wealth increased to the same degree as that of marketable wealth between 1983 and 1989. The share of the top 1 percent of financial wealth holders increased by 4 percentage points, from 43 to 47 percent of total financial wealth. The share of the next 19 percent fell from 48 to 46 percent, while that of the bottom 80 percent declined from 9 to 7 percent. Between 1989 and 1998, the share of total financial wealth of the top 1 percent increased a bit more (by 0.4 percentage points) but the share of the bottom 80 percent recovered to where it was in 1983.

Income distribution, too, became more concentrated between 1983 and 1989. As with wealth, most of the relative income gain accrued to the top 1 percent of recipients, whose share of total household income grew by 4 percentage points, from 13 to 17 percent. The share of the next 19 percent remained unchanged at 39 percent. Almost all the (relative) loss in income was sustained by the bottom 80 percent of the income distribution, whose share fell from 48 to 44 percent. Between 1989 and 1998, income inequality increased a bit more. While the share of the top 1 percent remained stable, the share of the next 19 percent rose by 0.6 percentage points and that of the bottom 80 percent correspondingly fell by 0.6 percentage points.

Another way to view rising wealth concentration is to look at how the increases in total wealth were divided over a specified period. This is calculated by dividing the increase in wealth of each group by the total increase in household wealth. The results for 1983-98, shown in Figure 4, indicate that the top 1 percent of wealth holders received 53 percent of the total gain in marketable wealth over the period. The next 19 percent received 38 percent, while the bottom 80 percent received only 9 percent. This pattern represents a distinct turnaround from the 1962-83 period, when every group enjoyed some share of the overall wealth growth and the gains were roughly in proportion to the share of wealth held by each in 1962. Over this period, the top 1 percent received 34 percent of the wealth gains, the next 19 percent claimed 48 percent, and the bottom 80 percent got 18 percent.

Figure 4
Percentage of Real Wealth (Income) Growth Accruing to Each Percentile Group, 1983-1998

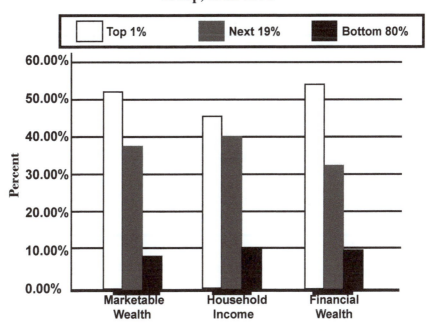

Source: 1960 and 1998 Survey of Consumer Finances

Gains in the overall growth in financial wealth were also distributed unevenly, with 56 percent of the growth accruing to the top 1 percent and 33 percent to the next 19 percent. The bottom 80 percent gained only 11 percent.

Finally, the changes in wealth distribution can be assessed by looking at the Gini coefficient. This indicator is used commonly to summarize data on the degree of inequality of income, wealth, or anything else of value. It ranges from 0 (exact equality) to 1 (one person owns everything); a higher Gini coefficient means greater inequality. This measure, like the others reviewed here, points to an increase in inequality. Between 1983 and 1989, the Gini coefficient increased from 0.80 to 0.84, between 1989 and 1998, the Gini coefficient remained at this high plateau.

Table 1
Number of Millionaires and Multimillionaires, 1983-1998 in 1000s

YEAR	TOTAL NUMBER OF HOUSEHOLDS	NUMBER OF HOUSEHOLDS WITH NET WORTH EQUAL TO OR EXCEEDING		
		$1,000,000	$5,000,000	$10,000,000
1983	83,893	2,411	247.0	66.5
1989	93,009	3,024	296.6	64.9
1992	95,462	3,104	277.4	41.6
1995	99,101	3,015	474.1	190.4
1998	102,547	4,783	755.5	239.4
PERCENT CHANGE:				
1983-1989	10.9%	25.4%	20.1%	-2.4%
1989-1998	10.3%	58.2%	154.7%	269.%

A. 1998 DOLLARS

Source: 1983, 1989, 1992, 1995, and 1998 Survey of Consumer Finances,
Federal Reserve Board of Washington, D.C.

The increase in wealth inequality recorded over the 1983-98 period—particularly between 1983 and 1989—in the United States is almost unprecedented. The only other period in the twentieth century during which concentration of household wealth rose comparably was from 1922 to 1929. Then, inequality was buoyed primarily by the excessive increase in stock values, which eventually crashed in 1929, leading to the Great Depression of the 1930s.

Despite the seemingly modest increase in overall wealth inequality during the 1990s, the decade witnessed a near explosion in the number of very rich households (see Table 1). The number of millionaires climbed by 54 percent between 1989 and 1998, the number of "pentamillionaires" ($5,000,000 or more) more than doubled, and the number of "decamillionaires" ($10,000,000 or more) almost quadrupled. Much of the growth occurred between 1995 and 1998 and was directly related to the surge in stock prices.

Consider Figure 3, the bar graph that visually documents the percentage of wealth as divided between the top 1%, the next 19%, and the bottom 80% (page 72). How do these visual images complicate the common linguistic phrase "middle class." Who is in the "middle class," and how much wealth would you assume that they have? How does the "middle" of the chart trouble conventional wisdom about the middle class? Are these definitions significant in terms of political conversations about "tax cuts for the rich" and/or "help for the middle class"?

It is hard to deny the fact of economic inequality in America today: according to the data from 1998 in Figure 3, the wealthiest 1% of Americans have nearly as much financial wealth as everyone else combined. But does "unequal" necessarily mean "unfair" or "unjust"? In your opinion, what factors would have to be taken into consideration to determine whether all these statistics represent an ethical or social problem?

A Nobel Prize winner in economics, Joseph E. Stiglitz is a former chief economist for the World Bank and Chair of the Council of Economic Advisors for the Clinton administration. He has written numerous books including Freefall: America, Free Markets, and the Sinking of the World Economy *and* Globalization and Its Discontents. *Stigitz remains an influential presence in modern economics. His opinion has been sought out by the Obama administration and the U.N. "Of the 1%, by the 1%, for the 1%" appeared in* Vanity Fair *magazine in May 2011.*

OF THE 1%, BY THE 1%, FOR THE 1%

BY JOSEPH E. STIGLITZ

It's no use pretending that what has obviously happened has not in fact happened. The upper 1 percent of Americans are now taking in nearly a quarter of the nation's income every year. In terms of wealth rather than income, the top 1 percent control 40 percent. Their lot in life has improved considerably. Twenty-five years ago, the corresponding figures were 12 percent and 33 percent. One response might be to celebrate the ingenuity and drive that brought good fortune to these people, and to contend that a rising tide lifts all boats. That response would be misguided. While the top 1 percent have seen their incomes rise 18 percent over the past decade, those in the middle have actually seen their incomes fall. For men with only high-school degrees, the decline has been precipitous—12 percent in the last quarter-century alone. All the growth in recent decades—and more—has gone to those at the top. In terms of income equality, America lags behind any country in the old, ossified Europe that President George W. Bush used to deride. Among our closest counterparts are Russia with its oligarchs and Iran. While many of the old centers of inequality in Latin America, such as Brazil, have been striving in recent years, rather successfully, to improve the plight of the poor and reduce gaps in income, America has allowed inequality to grow.

Economists long ago tried to justify the vast inequalities that seemed so troubling in the mid-19th century—inequalities that are but a pale shadow of what we are seeing in America today. The justification they came up with was called "marginal-productivity theory." In a nutshell, this theory associated higher incomes with higher productivity and a greater contribution to society. It is a theory that has always been cherished by the rich. Evidence for its validity, however, remains thin. The corporate executives who helped bring on the recession of the past three years—whose contribution to our society, and to their own companies, has been massively negative—went on to receive large bonuses. In some cases, companies were so embarrassed about calling such rewards "performance bonuses" that they felt compelled to change the name to "retention bonuses" (even if the only thing being retained was bad performance). Those who have contributed great positive innovations to our society, from the pioneers of genetic understanding to the pioneers of the Information Age, have received a pittance compared with those responsible for the financial innovations that brought our global economy to the brink of ruin.

Some people look at income inequality and shrug their shoulders. So what if this person gains and that person loses? What matters, they argue, is not how the pie is divided but the size of the pie. That argument is fundamentally wrong. An economy in which *most* citizens are doing worse year after year—an economy like America's—is not likely to do well over the long haul. There are several reasons for this.

First, growing inequality is the flip side of something else: shrinking opportunity. Whenever we diminish equality of opportunity, it means that we are not using some of our most valuable assets—our people—in the most productive way possible. Second, many of the distortions that lead to inequality—such as those associated with monopoly power and preferential tax treatment for special interests—undermine the efficiency of the economy. This new inequality goes on to create new distortions, undermining efficiency even further. To give just one example, far too many of our most talented young people, seeing the astronomical rewards, have gone into finance rather than into fields that would lead to a more productive and healthy economy.

Third, and perhaps most important, a modern economy requires "collective action"—it needs government to invest in infrastructure, education, and technology. The United States and the world have benefited greatly from government-sponsored research that led to the Internet, to advances in public health, and so on. But America has long suffered from an under-investment in infrastructure (look at the condition of our highways and bridges, our railroads and airports), in basic research, and in education at all levels. Further cutbacks in these areas lie ahead.

None of this should come as a surprise—it is simply what happens when a society's wealth distribution becomes lopsided. The more divided a society becomes in terms of wealth, the more reluctant the wealthy become to spend money on common needs. The rich don't need to rely on government for parks or education or medical care or personal security—they can buy all these things for themselves. In the process, they become more distant from ordinary people, losing whatever empathy they may once have had. They also worry about strong government—one that could use its powers to adjust the balance, take some of their wealth, and invest it for the common good. The top 1 percent may complain about the kind of government we have in America, but in truth they like it just fine: Too gridlocked to re-distribute, too divided to do anything but lower taxes.

Economists are not sure how to fully explain the growing inequality in America. The ordinary dynamics of supply and demand have certainly played a role: laborsaving technologies have reduced the demand for many "good" middle-class, blue-collar jobs. Globalization has created a worldwide marketplace, pitting expensive unskilled workers in America against cheap unskilled workers overseas. Social changes have also played a role—for instance, the decline of unions, which once represented a third of American workers and now represent about 12 percent.

But one big part of the reason we have so much inequality is that the top 1 percent want it that way. The most obvious example involves tax policy. Lowering tax rates on capital gains, which is how the rich receive a large portion of their income, has given the wealthiest Americans close to a free ride. Monopolies and near monopolies have always been a source of economic power—from John D. Rockefeller at the beginning of the last century to Bill Gates at the end. Lax enforcement of anti-trust laws, especially during Republican administrations, has been a godsend to the top 1 percent. Much of today's inequality is due to manipulation of the financial system, enabled by changes in the rules that have been bought and paid for by the financial industry itself—one of its best investments ever. The government lent money to financial institutions at close to 0 percent interest and provided generous bailouts on favorable terms when all else failed. Regulators turned a blind eye to a lack of transparency and to conflicts of interest.

When you look at the sheer volume of wealth controlled by the top 1 percent in this country, it's tempting to see our growing inequality as a quintessentially American achievement—we started way behind the pack, but now we're doing inequality on a world-class level. And it looks as if we'll be building on this achievement for years to come, because what made it possible is self-reinforcing. Wealth begets power, which begets more wealth. During the savings-and-loan scandal of the 1980s—a scandal whose dimensions, by today's standards, seem almost quaint—the banker Charles Keating was asked by a congressional committee whether the $1.5 million he had spread among a few key elected officials could actually buy influence. "I certainly hope so," he replied. The Supreme Court, in its recent *Citizens United* case, has enshrined the right of corporations to buy government, by removing limitations on campaign spending. The personal and the political are today in perfect alignment. Virtually all U.S. senators, and most of the representatives in the House, are members of the top 1 percent when they arrive, are kept in office by money from the top 1 percent, and know that if they serve the top 1 percent well they will be rewarded by the top 1 percent when they leave office. By and large, the key executive-branch policymakers on trade and economic policy also come from the top 1 percent. When pharmaceutical companies receive a trillion-dollar gift—through legislation prohibiting the government, the largest buyer of drugs, from bargaining over price—it should not come as cause for wonder. It should not make jaws drop that a tax bill cannot emerge from Congress unless big tax cuts are put in place for the wealthy. Given the power of the top 1 percent, this is the way you would *expect* the system to work.

America's inequality distorts our society in every conceivable way. There is, for one thing, a well-documented lifestyle effect—people outside the top 1 percent increasingly live beyond their means. Trickle-down economics may be a chimera, but trickle-down behaviorism is very real. Inequality massively distorts our foreign policy. The top 1 percent rarely serve in the military—the reality is that the "all-volunteer" army does not pay enough to attract their sons and daughters, and patriotism goes only so far. Plus, the wealthiest class feels no pinch from higher taxes when the nation goes to war: borrowed money will pay for all that. Foreign policy, by definition, is about the balancing of national interests and national resources. With the top 1 percent in charge, and paying no price, the notion of balance and restraint goes out the window. There is no limit to the adventures we can undertake; corporations and contractors stand only to gain. The rules of economic globalization are likewise designed to benefit the rich: they encourage competition among countries for *business*, which drives down taxes on corporations, weakens health and environmental protections, and undermines what used to be viewed as the "core" labor rights, which include the right to collective bargaining. Imagine what the world might look like if the rules were designed instead to encourage competition among countries for *workers*. Governments would compete in providing economic security, low taxes on ordinary wage earners, good education, and a clean environment—things workers care about. But the top 1 percent don't need to care.

Or, more accurately, they think they don't. Of all the costs imposed on our society by the top 1 percent, perhaps the greatest is this: the erosion of our sense of identity, in which fair play, equality of opportunity, and a sense of community are so important. America has long prided itself on being a fair society, where everyone has an equal chance of getting ahead, but the statistics suggest otherwise: the chances of a poor citizen, or even a middle-class citizen, making it to the top in America are smaller than in many countries of Europe. The cards are stacked against them. It is this sense of an unjust system without opportunity that has given rise to the conflagrations in the Middle East: Rising food prices and growing and persistent youth unemployment simply served as kindling. With youth unemployment in America at around 20 percent (and in some locations, and among some socio-demographic groups, at twice that); with one out of six Americans desiring a full-time job not able to get one; with one out of seven Americans on food stamps (and about the same number suffering from "food insecurity")—given all this, there is ample evidence that something has blocked the vaunted "trickling down" from the top 1 percent to everyone else. All of this is having the predictable effect of creating alienation—voter turnout among those in their 20s in the last election stood at 21 percent, comparable to the unemployment rate.

In recent weeks we have watched people taking to the streets by the millions to protest political, economic, and social conditions in the oppressive societies they inhabit. Governments have been toppled in Egypt and Tunisia. Protests have erupted in Libya, Yemen, and Bahrain. The ruling families elsewhere in the region look on nervously from their air-conditioned penthouses—will they be next? They are right to worry. These are societies where a minuscule fraction of the population—less than 1 percent—controls the lion's share of the wealth; where wealth is a main determinant of power; where entrenched corruption of one sort or another is a way of life; and where the wealthiest often stand actively in the way of policies that would improve life for people in general.

As we gaze out at the popular fervor in the streets, one question to ask ourselves is this: When will it come to America? In important ways, our own country has become like one of these distant, troubled places.

Alexis de Tocqueville once described what he saw as a chief part of the peculiar genius of American society—something he called "self-interest properly understood." The last two words were the key. Everyone possesses self-interest in a narrow sense: I want what's good for me right now! Self-interest "properly understood" is different. It means appreciating that paying attention to everyone else's self-interest—in other words, the common welfare—is in fact a precondition for one's own ultimate well-being. Tocqueville was not suggesting that there was anything noble or idealistic about this outlook—in fact, he was suggesting the opposite. It was a mark of American pragmatism. Those canny Americans understood a basic fact: looking out for the other guy isn't just good for the soul—it's good for business.

The top 1 percent have the best houses, the best educations, the best doctors, and the best lifestyles, but there is one thing that money doesn't seem to have bought: an understanding that their fate is bound up with how the other 99 percent live. Throughout history, this is something that the top 1 percent eventually do learn. Too late.

Stiglitz, having worked for the Clinton and Obama administrations, is probably somewhere left of the political center in his ideology. His critical stance toward globalization and free-market fundamentalism gives this characterization even more credence. Assuming that he is writing from a politically interested position, what might a conservative or neo-liberal economist take away from the same statistics regarding inequalities in wealth and income distribution?

Although not expressly stated by Stiglitz, other economists have asserted that severe inequality in income distribution is reminiscent of the feudal states of medieval Europe. Research the economies of feudal societies and critique this statement as either a true or false proposition.

This is a difficult topic. In a journal entry or blog post work through your ideas about income and wealth distribution inequality especially as your thinking has been supplemented by the invention and exploration activities.

Known as the "father of American music," Stephen Collins Foster is the writer of such standards as "Camptown Races," "My Old Kentucky Home," and "Oh! Susanna." The song "Hard Times" has been covered by numerous artists since the 19th century and was most recently and poignantly sung by Mary J. Blige during Hope for Haiti Now: A Global Benefit for Earthquake Relief.

HARD TIMES COME AGAIN NO MORE

BY STEPHEN C. FOSTER

Let us pause in life's pleasures and count its many tears,
while we all sup sorrow with the poor;
there's a song that will linger forever in our ears:
"Oh, hard times come again no more."

(Chorus)
'Tis the song, the sigh of the weary,
hard times, hard times, come again no more.
Many days you have lingered around my cabin door;
Oh, hard times come again no more.

While we seek mirth and beauty and music light and gay,
there are frail forms fainting at the door;
though their voices are silent, their pleading looks will say,
"Oh, hard times come again no more."

There's a pale drooping maiden who toils her life away,
with a worn heart whose better days are o'er;
though her voice would be merry, 'tis sighing all the day,
"Oh, hard times come again no more."

'Tis a sigh that is wafted across the troubled wave,
'tis a wail that is heard upon the shore,
'tis a dirge that is murmured around the lowly grave,
"Oh, hard times come again no more."

Think about your reaction to seeing homeless people with signs at intersections or in parking lots asking passersby to give them money. Think about your reaction to panhandlers on the sidewalks. What do you initially think? What is your emotional reaction?

Research the website for the National Coalition for the Homeless (http://nationalhomeless.org) or the site for the U.S. Department of Housing and Urban Development (http://portal.hud.gov/hudportal/HUD?src=/topics/homelessness). What are the statistics about homelessness and how have they changed since the financial crash in 2008? What do the homeless experience according to these sites?

Compare the results of the previous two activities. Reflect on any changes in your perception of the homeless or homelessness in general.

In a group, list what adversities you think poor people face in different locations. What do the urban poor face? The rural poor? The suburban poor? What about poverty in other nations—from ones with relatively stable governments to ones that are war torn? Share your list with the class as a whole.

John Scalzi is a freelance writer based in Bedford, Ohio. He has written numerous works of both fiction and nonfiction and is the president of the Science Fiction & Fantasy Writers of America. "Being Poor" appears on his website, Whatever <http://scalzi.com>. The readers' comments on this piece are extensive and well worth reading as they add many, many lines to the original Scalzi piece.

BEING POOR

BY JOHN SCALZI

Being poor is knowing exactly how much everything costs.

Being poor is getting angry at your kids for asking for all the crap they see on TV.

Being poor is having to keep buying $800 cars because they're what you can afford, and then having the cars break down on you, because there's not an $800 car in America that's worth a damn.

Being poor is hoping the toothache goes away.

Being poor is knowing your kid goes to friends' houses but never has friends over to yours.

Being poor is going to the restroom before you get in the school lunch line so your friends will be ahead of you and won't hear you say "I get free lunch" when you get to the cashier.

Being poor is living next to the freeway.

Being poor is coming back to the car with your children in the back seat, clutching that box of Raisin Bran you just bought and trying to think of a way to make the kids understand that the box has to last.

Being poor is wondering if your well-off sibling is lying when he says he doesn't mind when you ask for help.

Being poor is off-brand toys.

Being poor is a heater in only one room of the house.

Being poor is knowing you can't leave $5 on the coffee table when your friends are around.

Being poor is hoping your kids don't have a growth spurt.

Being poor is stealing meat from the store, frying it up before your mom gets home and then telling her she doesn't have to make dinner tonight because you're not hungry anyway.

Being poor is Goodwill underwear.

Being poor is not enough space for everyone who lives with you.

Being poor is feeling the glued soles tear off your supermarket shoes when you run around the playground.

Being poor is your kid's school being the one with the 15-year-old textbooks and no air conditioning.

Being poor is thinking $8 an hour is a really good deal.

Being poor is relying on people who don't give a damn about you.

Being poor is an overnight shift under florescent lights.

Being poor is finding the letter your mom wrote to your dad, begging him for the child support.

Being poor is a bathtub you have to empty into the toilet.

Being poor is stopping the car to take a lamp from a stranger's trash.

Being poor is making lunch for your kid when a cockroach skitters over the bread, and you looking over to see if your kid saw.

Being poor is believing a GED actually makes a goddamned difference.

Being poor is people angry at you just for walking around in the mall.

Being poor is not taking the job because you can't find someone you trust to watch your kids.

Being poor is the police busting into the apartment right next to yours.

Being poor is not talking to that girl because she'll probably just laugh at your clothes.

Being poor is hoping you'll be invited for dinner.

Being poor is a sidewalk with lots of brown glass on it.

Being poor is people thinking they know something about you by the way you talk.

Being poor is needing that 35-cent raise.

Being poor is your kid's teacher assuming you don't have any books in your home.

Being poor is six dollars short on the utility bill and no way to close the gap.

Being poor is crying when you drop the mac and cheese on the floor.

Being poor is knowing you work as hard as anyone, anywhere.

Being poor is people surprised to discover you're not actually stupid.

Being poor is people surprised to discover you're not actually lazy.

Being poor is a six-hour wait in an emergency room with a sick child asleep on your lap.

Being poor is never buying anything someone else hasn't bought first.

Being poor is picking the 10 cent ramen instead of the 12 cent ramen because that's two extra packages for every dollar.

Being poor is having to live with choices you didn't know you made when you were 14 years old.

Being poor is getting tired of people wanting you to be grateful.

Being poor is knowing you're being judged.

Being poor is a box of crayons and a $1 coloring book from a community center Santa.

Being poor is checking the coin return slot of every soda machine you go by.

Being poor is deciding that it's all right to base a relationship on shelter.

Being poor is knowing you really shouldn't spend that buck on a Lotto ticket.

Being poor is hoping the register lady will spot you the dime.

Being poor is feeling helpless when your child makes the same mistakes you did, and won't listen to you beg them against doing so.

Being poor is a cough that doesn't go away.

Being poor is making sure you don't spill on the couch, just in case you have to give it back before the lease is up.

Being poor is a $200 paycheck advance from a company that takes $250 when the paycheck comes in.

Being poor is four years of night classes for an Associates of Art degree.

Being poor is a lumpy futon bed.

Being poor is knowing where the shelter is.

Being poor is people who have never been poor wondering why you choose to be so.

Being poor is knowing how hard it is to stop being poor.

Being poor is seeing how few options you have.

Being poor is running in place.

Being poor is people wondering why you didn't leave.

Which one of Scalzi's statements about being poor do you find the most affecting, and which the least? Why? Does your reaction tell you something about your own beliefs regarding things that should be considered rights and things considered privileges? What material aspects of life do you consider expendable, and what things seem dehumanizing in their absence?

In your small group, collect Scalzi's statements into general categories. You might consider the items that deal with material discomfort separately from those explicitly about parenting, for instance. Then, together, analyze one group of statements: How do these ideas collectively express an opinion on some ethical aspect of society, the rights of man and the wrongs of economic inequality? Is this an opinion that your group can debate? On what grounds?

Issues of honesty and trust arise in several of Scalzi's statements. How is "being poor" linked to demonstrating moral or ethical behavior, or expecting it from the people around you? Is this relationship between poverty and ethics common, inevitable, overstated? Write a paragraph in which you explore how morals and poverty might come into conflict.

Scalzi says that "being poor is seeing how few options you have." What options are there for the poor in your community? What qualifications or other factors need to be in place for poor people to survive, "leave," or rise?

Barbara Ehrenreich is the bestselling author of many books including Bait and Switch: The (Futile) Pursuit of the American Dream, Bright-sided: How the Relentless Promotion of Positive Thinking Has Undermined America, *and* 2001's Nickel and Dimed: On (Not) Getting By in America, *from which this excerpt is taken. In* Nickel and Dimed *Ehrenreich chronicles her journey into the life of America's low-wage workers.*

SERVING IN FLORIDA

BY BARBARA EHRENREICH

Mostly out of laziness, I decide to start my low-wage life in the town nearest to where I actually live, Key West, Florida, which with a population of about 25,000 is elbowing its way up to the status of a genuine city. The downside of familiarity, I soon realize, is that it's not easy to go from being a consumer, thoughtlessly throwing money around in exchange for groceries and movies and gas, to being a worker in the very same place. I am terrified, especially at the beginning, of being recognized by some friendly business owner or erstwhile neighbor and having to stammer out some explanation of my project. Happily, though, my fears turn out to be entirely unwarranted: during the month of poverty and toil, no one recognizes my face or my name, which goes unnoticed and for the most part unuttered. In this parallel universe where my father never got out of the mines and I never got through college, I am "baby," "honey," "blondie," and, most commonly, "girl."

My first task is to find a place to live. I figure that if I can earn $7 an hour—which, from the want ads, seems doable—I can afford to spend $500 on rent or maybe, with severe economies, $600 and still have $400 or $500 left over for food and gas. In the Key West area, this pretty much confines me to flophouses and trailer homes—like the one, a pleasing fifteen minute drive from town, that has no air-conditioning, no screens, no fans, no television, and, by the way of diversion, only the challenge of evading the landlord's Doberman Pinscher. The big problem with this place, though, is the rent, which at $675 a month is well beyond my reach. All right, Key West is expensive. But so is New York

City, or the Bay Area, or Jackson, Wyoming, or Telluride, or Boston, or any other place where tourists and the wealthy compete for living space with the people who clean their toilets and fry their hash browns. Still, it is a shock to realize that "trailer trash" has become, for me, a demographic category to aspire to.

So I decide to make the common trade-off between affordability and convenience and go for a $500-a-month "efficiency" thirty miles up a two-lane highway from the employment opportunities of Key West, meaning forty-five minutes if there's no road construction and I don't get caught behind some sun-dazed Canadian tourists. I hate the drive, along a roadside studded with white crosses commemorating the more effective head-on collisions, but it's a sweet little place—a cabin, more or less, set in the swampy backyard of the converted mobile home where my landlord, an affable TV repairman, lives with his bartender girlfriend. Anthropologically speaking, the trailer park would be preferable, but here I have a gleaming white floor and a firm mattress, and the few resident bugs are easily vanquished.

The next piece of business is to comb through the want ads and find a job. I rule out various occupations for one reason or another: hotel front-desk clerk, for example, which to my surprise is regarded as unskilled and pays only $6 or $7 an hour, gets eliminated because it involves standing in one spot for eight hours a day. Waitressing is also something I'd like to avoid, because I remember it leaving me bone-tired when I was eighteen, and I'm decades of varicosities and back pain beyond that now. Telemarketing, one of the first refuges of the suddenly indigent, can be dismissed on grounds of personality. This leaves certain supermarket jobs, such as deli clerk, or housekeeping in the hotels and guest houses, which pays about $7 and, I imagine, is not too different from what I've been doing part-time, in my own home, all my life.

So I put on what I take to be a respectable-looking outfit of ironed Bermuda shorts and scooped-neck T-shirt and set out for a tour of the local hotels and supermarkets. Best Western, Econo Lodge, and HoJo's all let me fill out application forms, and these are, to my relief, mostly interested in whether I am a legal resident of the United States and have committed any felonies. My next stop is Winn-Dixie, the supermarket, which turns out to have a particularly onerous application process, featuring a twenty-minute "interview" by computer since, apparently, no human on the premises is deemed capable of representing the corporate point of view. I am conducted to a large room decorated with posters illustrating how to look "professional" (it helps to be white and, if female, permed) and warning of the slick promises that union organizers might try to tempt me with. The interview is multiple-choice: Do I have anything, such as child care problems, that might make it hard for me to get to work on time? Do I think safety on the job is the responsibility of management? Then, popping up cunningly out of the blue: How many dollars' worth of stolen goods have I purchased in the last year? Would I turn in a fellow employee if I caught him stealing? Finally, "Are you an honest person?"

Apparently I ace the interview, because I am told that all I have to do is show up in some doctor's office tomorrow for a urine test. This seems to be a fairly general rule: If you want to stack Cheerios boxes or vacuum hotel rooms in chemically fascist America, you have to be willing to squat down and pee in front of a health worker (who has no doubt had to do the same thing herself.)[1] The wages Winn-Dixie is offering—$6 and a couple of dimes to start with— are not enough, I decide, to compensate for this indignity.

I lunch at Wendy's, where $4.99 gets you unlimited refills at the Mexican part of the Super-bar, a comforting surfeit of refried beans and cheese sauce. A teenage employee, seeing me studying the want ads, kindly offers me an application form, which I fill out, though here, too, the pay is just $6 and change an hour. Then it's off for a round of the locally owned inns and guest houses in Key West's Old Town, which is where all the serious sightseeing and guzzling goes on, a couple of miles removed from the functional end of the island, where the discount hotels make their homes. At The Palms, let's call it, a bouncy manager actually takes me around to see the rooms and meet the current housekeepers, who, I note with satisfaction, look pretty much like me—faded ex-hippie types in shorts with long hair pulled back in braids. Mostly, though, no one speaks to me or even looks at me except to proffer an application form. At my last stop, a palatial B & B, I wait twenty minutes to meet "Max," only to be told that there are no jobs now but there should be one soon, since "nobody lasts more than a couple weeks."

---

1 Eighty-one percent of large employers now require preemployment drug testing, up from 21 percent in 1987. Among all employers, the rate of testing is highest in the South. The drug most likely to be detected—marijuana, which can be detected weeks after use—is also the most innocuous, while heroin and cocaine are generally undetectable three days after use. Alcohol, which clears the body within hours after ingestion, is not tested for.

Three days go by like this and, to my chagrin, no one from the approximately twenty places at which I've applied calls me for an interview. I had been vain enough to worry about coming across as too educated for the jobs I sought, but no one even seems interested in finding out how overqualified I am. Only later will I realize that the want ads are not a reliable measure of the actual jobs available at any particular time. They are, as I should have guessed from Max's comment, the employers' insurance policy against the relentless turnover of the low-wage workforce. Most of the big hotels run ads almost continually, if only to build a supply of applicants to replace the current workers as they drift away or are fired, so finding a job is just a matter of being in the right place at the right time and flexible enough to take whatever is being offered that day. This finally happens to me at one of the big discount chain hotels where I go, as usual, for housekeeping and am sent instead to try out as a waitress at the attached "family restaurant," a dismal spot looking out on a parking garage, which is featuring " Polish sausage and BBQ sauce" on this 95-degree day. Phillip, the dapper young West Indian who introduces himself as the manager, interviews me with about as much enthusiasm as if he were a clerk processing me for Medicare, the principal questions being what shifts I can work and when I can start. I mutter about being woefully out of practice as a waitress, but he's already on to the uniform: I'm to show up tomorrow wearing black slacks and black shoes; he'll provide the rust-colored polo shirt with "Hearthside," as we'll call the place, embroidered on it, though I might want to wear my own shirt to get to work, haha. At the word *tomorrow*, something between fear and indignation rises in my chest. I want to say, "Thank you for your time, sir, but this is just an experiment, you know, not my actual life."

SO BEGINS MY CAREER AT THE HEARTHSIDE, WHERE FOR TWO WEEKS I work from 2:00 till 10:00 p.m. for $2.43 an hour plus tips.[2] Employees are barred from using the front door, so I enter the first day through the kitchen, where a red-faced man with shoulder-length blond hair is throwing frozen steaks against the wall and yelling, "Fuck this shit!" "That's just Billy," explains Gail, the wiry middle-aged waitress who is assigned to train me. "He's on the rag again"—a condition occasioned, in this instance,

---

2 According to the Fair Labor Standards Act, employers are not required to pay "tipped employees," such as restaurant servers, more than $2.13 an hour in direct wages. However, if the sum of tips plus $2.13 an hour falls below the minimum wage, or $5.15 an hour, the employer is required to make up the difference. This fact was not mentioned by managers or otherwise publicized at either of the restaurants where I worked.

by the fact that the cook on the morning shift had forgotten to thaw out the steaks. For the next eight hours, I run after the agile Gail, absorbing bits of instructions along with fragments of personal tragedy. All food must be trayed, and the reason she's so tired today is that she woke up in a cold sweat thinking of her boyfriend, who was killed a month ago in a scuffle in an upstate prison. No refills on lemonade. And the reason he was in prison is that a few DUIs caught up with him, that's all, could have happened to anyone. Carry the creamers to the table in a "monkey bowl," never in your hand. And after he was gone she spent several months living in her truck, peeing in a plastic pee bottle and reading by candlelight at night, but you can't live in a truck in the summer, since you need to have the windows down, which means anything can get in, from mosquitoes on up.

At least Gail puts to rest any fears I had of appearing overqualified. From the first day on, I find that of all the things that I have left behind, such as home and identity, what I miss the most is competence. Not that I have ever felt 100 percent competent in the writing business, where one day's success augurs nothing at all for the next. But in my writing life, I at least have some notion of *procedure:* do the research, make the outline, rough out a draft, etc. As a server, though, I am beset by requests as if by bees: more iced tea here, catsup over there, a to-go box for table 14, and where are the high chairs, anyway? Of the twenty-seven tables, up to six are usually mine at any time, though on slow afternoons or if Gail is off, I sometimes have the whole place to myself. There is the touch-screen computer-ordering system to master, which I suppose is meant to minimize server-cook contacts but in practice requires constant verbal fine-tuning: "That's gravy on the mashed, OK? None on the meatloaf," and so forth. Plus, something I had forgotten in the years since I was eighteen: About a third of a server's job is "side work" invisible to customers—sweeping, scrubbing, slicing, refilling, and restocking. If it isn't all done, every little bit of it, you're going to face the 6:00 P.M. dinner rush defenseless and probably go down in flames. I screw up dozens of times at the beginning, sustained in my shame entirely by Gail's support—"It's OK, baby, everyone does that sometime"—because, to my total surprise and despite the scientific detachment I am doing my best to maintain, I *care*.

The whole thing would be a lot easier if I could just skate through it like Lily Tomlin in one of her waitress skits, but I was raised by the absurd Booker T. Washingtonian precept that says: If you're going to do something, do it well. In fact, "well" isn't good enough by half. Do it better than anyone has ever done it before. Or so said my father, who must have known what he was talking about because he managed to pull himself, and us with him, up from the mile-deep copper mines of Butte to the leafy suburbs of the Northeast, ascending from boilermakers to martinis before booze beat out ambition. As in most endeavors I have encountered in my life, "doing it better than anyone" is not a reasonable goal. Still, when I wake up at 4 a.m. in my own cold sweat, I am not thinking about the writing deadlines I'm neglecting; I'm thinking of the table where I screwed up the order and one of the kids didn't get his kiddie meal until the rest of the family had moved on to their Key lime pies. That's the other powerful motivation—the customers, or "patients," as I can't help thinking of them on account of the mysterious vulnerability that seems to have left them temporarily unable to feed themselves. After a few days at Hearthside, I feel the service ethic kick in like a shot of oxytocin, the nurturance hormone. The plurality of my customers are hardworking locals— truck drivers, construction workers, even housekeepers from the attached hotel—and I want them to have the closest to a "fine dining" experience that the grubby circumstances will allow. No "you guys" for me; everyone over twelve is "sir" or "ma'am." I ply them with iced tea and coffee refills; I return, midmeal, to inquire how everything is; I doll up their salads with chopped raw mushrooms, summer squash slices, or whatever bits of produce I can find that have survived their sojourn in the cold storage room mold-free.

There is Benny, for example, a short, tight-muscled sewer repairman who cannot even think of eating until he has absorbed a half hour of air-conditioning and ice water. We chat about hyperthermia and electrolytes until he is ready to order some finicky combination like soup of the day, garden salad, and a side of grits. There are the German tourists who are so touched by my pidgin *"Wilkommen"* and *"Ist alles gut?"* that they actually tip. (Europeans, no doubt spoiled by their trade union-ridden, high-wage welfare states, generally do not know that they are supposed to tip. Some restaurants, the Hearthside included, allow servers to "grat" their foreign customers, or add a tip to the bill. Since this amount is added before the customers have a chance to tip or not tip, the practice amounts to an automatic penalty for imperfect English.) There are the two dirt-smudged lesbians, just off from their shift, who are impressed enough by my suave handling of the fly in the pina colada that they take the time to praise me to Stu, the assistant manager. There's Sam, the kindly retired cop who has to plug up his tracheotomy hole with one finger in order to force the cigarette smoke into his lungs.

Sometimes I play with the fantasy that I am a princess who, in penance for some tiny transgression, has undertaken to feed each of her subjects by hand. But the nonprincesses working with me are just as indulgent, even when this means flouting management rules—as to, for example, the number of croutons that can go on a salad (six). "Put on all you want," Gail whispers, "as long as Stu isn't looking." She dips into her own tip money to buy biscuits and gravy for an out-of-work mechanic who's used up all his money on dental surgery, inspiring me to pick up the tab for his pie and milk. Maybe the same high levels of agape can be found throughout the "hospitality industry." I remember the poster decorating one of the apartments I looked at, which said, "If you seek happiness for yourself you will never find it. Only when you seek happiness for others will it come to you," or words to that effect—an odd sentiment, it seemed to me at the time, to find in the dank one-room basement apartment of a bellhop at the Best Western. At Hearthside, we utilize whatever bits of autonomy we have to ply our customers with the illicit calories that signal our love. It is our job as servers to assemble the salads and desserts, pour the dressings, and squirt the whipped cream. We also control the number of butter pats our customers get and the amount of sour cream on their baked potatoes. So if you wonder why Americans are so obese, consider the fact that waitresses both express their humanity and earn their tips through the covert distribution of fats.

Ten days into it, this is beginning to look like a livable lifestyle. I like Gail, who is "looking at fifty," agewise, but moves so fast she can alight in one place and then another without apparently being anywhere between. I clown around with Lionel, the teenage Haitian dishwashers' musical Creole, which sounds, in their rich bass voices, like French on testosterone. I bond with Timmy, the fourteen-year-old white kid who buses at night, by telling him I don't like people putting their baby seats right on the tables: It makes the baby look too much like a side dish. He snickers delightedly and in return, on a slow night, starts telling me the plots of all the *Jaws* movies (which are perennial favorites in the shark-ridden Keys): "She looks around, and the water-skier isn't there anymore, then SNAP! The whole boat goes…"

I especially like Joan, the svelte fortyish hostess, who turns out to be a militant feminist, pulling me aside one day to explain that "men run everything—we don't have a chance unless we stick together." Accordingly, she backs me up when I get overpowered on the floor, and in return I give her a chunk of my tips or stand guard while she sneaks off for an unauthorized cigarette break. We all admire her for standing up to Billy and telling him, after some of his usual nastiness about the female server class, to "shut the fuck up." I even warm up to Billy when, on a slow night and to make up for a particularly unwarranted attack on my abilities, or so I imagine, he tells me about his glory days as a young man at "coronary school" in Brooklyn, where he dated a knockout Puerto Rican chick—or do you say "culinary"?

I finish up every night at 10:00 or 10:30, depending on how much side work I've been able to get done during the shift, and cruise home to the tapes I snatched at random when I left my real home—Marianne Faithfull, Tracy Chapman, Enigma, King Sunny Ade, Violent Femmes—just drained enough for the music to set my cranium resonating, but hardly dead. Midnight snack is Wheat Thins and Monterey Jack, accompanied by cheap white wine on ice and whatever AMC has to offer. To bed by 1:30 or 2:00, up at 9:00 or 10:00, read for an hour while my uniform whirls around in the landlord's washing machine, and then it's another eight hours spent following Mao's central instruction, as laid out in the Little Red Book, which was: Serve the people.

I could drift along like this, in some dreamy proletarian idyll, except for two things. One is management. If I have kept this subject to the margins so far it is because I still flinch to think that I spent all those weeks under the surveillance of men (and later women) whose job it was to monitor my behavior for signs of sloth, theft, drug abuse, or worse. Not that managers and especially "assistant managers" in low-wage settings like this are exactly the class enemy. Mostly, in the restaurant business, they are former cooks still capable of pinch-hitting in the kitchen, just as in hotels they are likely to be former clerks, and paid a salary of only about $400 a week. But everyone knows they have crossed over to the other side, which is, crudely put, corporate as opposed to human. Cooks want to prepare tasty meals, servers want to serve them graciously, but managers are there for only one reason—to make sure that money is made for some theoretical entity, the corporation, which exists far away in Chicago or New York, if a corporation can be said to have a physical existence at all. Reflecting on her career, Gail tells me ruefully that she swore, years ago, never to work for a corporation again. "They don't cut you no slack. You give and you give and they take."

Managers can sit—for hours at a time if they want—but it's their job to see that no one else ever does, even when there's nothing to do, and this is why, for servers, slow times can be as exhausting as rushes. You start dragging out each little chore because if the manager on duty catches you in an idle moment he will give you something far nastier to do. So I wipe, I clean, I consolidate catsup bottles and recheck the cheesecake supply, even tour the tables to make sure the customer evaluation forms are all standing perkily in their places—wondering all the time how many calories I burn in these strictly theatrical exercises. In desperation, I even take the desserts out of their glass display case and freshen them up with whipped cream and bright new maraschino cherries; anything to look busy. When, on a particularly dead afternoon, Stu finds me glancing at a *USA Today* a customer has left behind, he assigns me to vacuum the entire floor with the broken vacuum cleaner, which has a handle only two feet long, and the only way to do that without incurring orthopedic damage is to proceed from spot to spot on your knees.

On my first Friday at Hearthside there is a "mandatory meeting for all restaurant employees," which I attend, eager for insight into our overall marketing strategy and the niche (your basic Ohio cuisine with a tropical twist?) we aim to inhabit. But there is no "we" at this meeting. Phillip, our top manager except for an occasional "consultant" sent out by corporate headquarters, opens it with a sneer: "The break room—it's disgusting. Butts in the ashtrays, newspapers lying around, crumbs." This windowless little room, which also houses the time clock for the entire hotel, is where we stash our bags and civilian clothes and take our half-hour meal breaks. But a break room is not a right, he tells us, it can be taken away. We should also know that the lockers in the break room and whatever is in them can be searched at any time. Then comes gossip; there has been gossip; gossip (which seems to mean employees talking among themselves) must stop. Off-duty employees are henceforth barred from eating at the restaurant, because "other servers gather around them and gossip." When Phillip has exhausted his agenda of rebukes, Joan complains about the condition of the ladies' room and I throw in my two bits about the vacuum cleaner. But I don't see any backup coming from my fellow servers, each of whom has slipped into her own personal funk; Gail, my role model, stares sorrowfully at a point six inches from her nose. The meeting ends when Andy, one of the cooks, gets up, muttering about breaking up his day off for this almighty bullshit.

Just four days later we are suddenly summoned into the kitchen at 3:30 p.m., even though there are live tables on the floor. We all—about ten of us—stand around Phillip, who announces grimly that there has been a report of some "drug activity" on the night shift and that, as a result, we are now to be a "drug-free" workplace, meaning that all new hires will be tested and possibly also current employees on a random basis. I am glad that this part of the kitchen is so dark because I find myself blushing as hard as if I had been caught toking up in the ladies' room myself: I haven't been treated this way—lined up in the corridor, threatened with locker searches, peppered with carelessly aimed accusations—since at least junior high school. Back on the floor, Joan cracks, "Next they'll be telling us we can't have *sex* on the job." When I ask Stu what happened to inspire the crackdown, he just mutters about "management decisions" and takes the opportunity to upbraid Gail and me for being too generous with the rolls. From now on there's to be only one per customer and it goes out with the dinner, not with the salad. He's also been riding the cooks, prompting Andy to come out of the kitchen and observe—with the serenity of a man whose customary implement is a butcher knife—that "Stu has a death wish today."

Later in the evening, the gossip crystallizes around the theory that Stu is himself the drug culprit, that he uses the restaurant phone to order up marijuana and sends one of the late servers out to fetch it for him. The server was caught and she may have ratted out Stu, at least enough to cast some suspicion on him, thus accounting for his pissy behavior. Who knows? Personally, I'm ready to believe anything bad about Stu, who serves no evident function and presumes too much on our common ethnicity, sidling up to me one night to engage in a little nativism directed at the Haitian immigrants: "I feel like I'm the foreigner here. They're taking over the country." Still later that evening, the drug in question escalates to crack. Lionel, the busboy, entertains us for the rest of the shift by standing just behind Stu's back and sucking deliriously on an imaginary joint or maybe a pipe.

The other problem, in addition to the less-than-nurturing management style, is that this job shows no sign of being financially viable. You might imagine, from a comfortable distance, that people who live, year in and year out, on $6 to $10 an hour have discovered some survival strategems unknown to the middle class. But no. It's not hard to get my coworkers talking about their living situations, because housing, in almost every case, is the principal source of disruption on their lives, the first thing they fill you in on when they arrive for their shifts. After a week, I have compiled the following survey:

> Gail is sharing a room in a well-known downtown flophouse for $250 a week. Her roommate, a male friend, has begun hitting on her, driving her nuts, but the rent would be impossible alone.

> Claude, the Haitian cook, is desperate to get out of the two-room apartment he shares with his girlfriend and two other, unrelated people. As far as I can determine, the other Haitian men live in similarly crowded situations.

> Annette, a twenty-year-old server who is six months pregnant and abandoned by her boyfriend, lives with her mother, a postal clerk.

> Marianne, who is a breakfast server, and her boyfriend are paying $170 a week for a one-person trailer.

> Billy, who at $10 an hour is the wealthiest of us, lives in the trailer he owns, paying only the $400-a-month lot fee.

> The other white cook, Andy, lives on his dry-docked boat, which, as far as I can tell from his loving descriptions, can't be more than twenty feet long. He offers to take me out on it once it's repaired, but the offer comes with inquiries as to my marital status, so I do not follow up on it.

> Tina, another server, and her husband are paying $60 a night for a room in the Days Inn. This is because they have no car and the Days Inn is in walking distance of the Hearthside. When Marianne is tossed out of her trailer for subletting (which is against trailer park rules), she leaves her boyfriend and moves in with Tina and her husband.

> Joan, who had fooled me with her numerous and tasteful outfits (hostesses wear their own clothes), lives in a van parked behind a shopping center at night and showers in Tina's motel room. The clothes are from thrift shops.[3]

---

3   I could find no statistics on the number of employed people living in cars or vans, but according to a 1997 report of the National Coalition for the Homeless, "Myths and Facts about Homelessness," nearly one-fifth of all homeless people (in twenty-nine cities across the nation) are employed in full or part-time jobs.

It strikes me, in my middle-class solipsism, that there is gross improvidence in some of these arrangements. When Gail and I are wrapping silverware in napkins—the only task for which we are permitted to sit—she tells me she is thinking of escaping from her roommate by moving into the Days Inn herself. I am astounded: How she can even think of paying $40 to $60 a day? But if I was afraid of sounding like a social worker, I have come out just sounding like a fool. She squints at me in disbelief: "And where am I supposed to get a month's rent and a month's deposit for an apartment?" I'd been feeling pretty smug about my $500 efficiency, but of course it was made possible only by the $1,300 I had allotted myself for start-up costs when I began my low-wage life: $1,000 for the first month's rent and deposit, $100 for initial groceries and cash in my pocket, $200 stuffed away for emergencies. In poverty, as in certain propositions in physics, starting conditions are everything.

There are no secret economies that nourish the poor; on the contrary, there are a host of special costs. If you can't put up the two months' rent you need to secure an apartment, you end up paying through the nose for a room by the week. If you have only a room, with a hot plate at best, you can't save by cooking up huge lentil stews that can be frozen for the week ahead. You eat fast food or the hot dogs and Styrofoam cups of soup that can be microwaved in a convenience store. If you have no money for health insurance—and the Hearthside's niggardly plan kicks in only after three months—you go without routine care or prescription drugs and end up paying the price. Gail, for example, was doing fine, healthwise anyway, until she ran out of money for estrogen pills. She is supposed to be on the company health plan by now, but they claim to have lost her application form and to be beginning the paperwork all over again. So she spends $9 a pop for pills to control the migraines she wouldn't have, she insists, if her estrogen supplements were covered. Similarly, Marianne's boyfriend lost his job as a roofer because he missed so much time after getting a cut on his foot for which he couldn't afford the prescribed antibiotic.

My own situation, when I sit down to assess it after two weeks of work, would not be much better if this were my actual life. The seductive thing about waitressing is that you don't have to wait for payday to feel a few bills in your pocket, and my tips usually cover meals and gas, plus something left over to stuff into the kitchen drawer I use as a bank. But as the tourist business slows in the summer heat, I sometimes leave work with only $20 in tips (the gross is higher, but servers share about 15 percent of their tips with the busboys and bartenders). With wages included, this amounts to about the minimum wage of $5.15 an hour. The sum in the drawer is piling up but at the present rate of accumulation will be more than $100 short of my rent when the end of the month comes around. Nor can I see any expenses to cut. True, I haven't gone the lentil stew route yet, but that's because I don't have a large cooking pot, potholders, or a ladle to stir with (which would cost a total of about $30 at Kmart, somewhat less at a thrift store), not to mention onions, carrots, and the indispensable bay leaf. I do make my lunch almost everyday—usually some slow-burning, high-protein combo like frozen chicken patties with melted cheese on top and canned pinto beans on the side. Dinner is at the Hearthside, which offers its employees a choice of BLT, fish sandwich, or hamburger for only $2. The burger lasts longest, especially if it's heaped with gut-puckering jalapenos, but by midnight my stomach is growling again.

So unless I want to start using my car as a residence, I have to find a second or an alternative job. I call all the hotels I'd filled out housekeeping applications at weeks ago—the Hyatt, Holiday Inn, Econo Lodge, HoJo's, Best Western, plus a half dozen locally run guest houses. Nothing. Then I start making the rounds again, wasting whole mornings waiting for some assistant manager to show up, even dipping into places so creepy that the front-desk clerk greets you from behind bullet-proof glass and sells pints of liquor over the counter. But either someone has exposed my real-life housekeeping habits—which are, shall we say, mellow—or I am at the wrong end of some infallible ethnic equation: most, but by no means all, of the working housekeepers I see on my job searches are African Americans, Spanish-speaking, or refugees from the Central European post-Communist world, while servers are almost invariably white and monolingually English-speaking. When I finally get a positive response, I have been identified once again as server material. Jerry's—again, not the real name—which is part of a well-known national chain and physically attached here to another budget hotel, is ready to use me at once. The prospect is both exciting and terrifying because, with about the same number of tables and counter seats, Jerry's attracts three or four times the volume of customers as the gloomy old Hearthside.

Explore

Pick a city where you'd like to go and live for a while. Using the web (and current newspapers if you can get them), prepare a worksheet that analyzes wages and the cost of living. In the want-ads, find jobs for which you might be qualified and that you'd be willing to perform. Online, or by phone, price apartments, considering not only their size but their amenities, utilities, and neighborhoods. Consider other "necessities" of life: insurance, transportation, healthcare, food, recreation. What would your work buy, and how much would you have to work for the lifestyle you want?

Invent

Ehrenreich tells of a co-worker making the seemingly ridiculous decision to spend as much as $60 per night to live at the Days Inn because she doesn't have the "start-up" money for an apartment. She herself finds cutting food costs impossible without a pot, a ladle, or potholders, not to mention ingredients to make lentil soup. Considering all the "start-up" costs, the consumables, and the things paid for by others, how much does a day in your life cost? Keep an inventory for 24 hours. Imagine ways that a person like Tina, living in her hotel room between waitressing shifts, could get started.

Compose

What Ehrenreich finds amidst her minimum wage job experiment is not just how difficult it is to live without money but how in this world of work her old self is challenged, changed, erased, and resilient. Describe the personal aspects of a job you've had. How did the work—the physicality, the community, the behavioral expectations, the hiring and review process, etc.—affect your personality, or how did your personality affect your experience on the job?

Collaborate

In a small group, analyze and critique Ehrenreich's experiment. Do you think she could have done some things differently to achieve a more favorable conclusion? What could she have changed? What factors might have made her experience easier than another person's similar situation? On the other hand, what factors could have made an experience like hers more difficult—even impossible for someone else to survive?

A professor of sociology at Princeton University, Viviana Zelizer is particularly interested in how economics affects social relationships. She has written about the "economic and sentimental value of children," as well as how money affects personal and intimate relationships. "A Dollar of Her Own" is taken from her 1994 book, The Social Meaning of Money and looks at the intersection economics and domestic politics.

A DOLLAR OF HER OWN

BY VIVIANA ZELIZER

DEFINING WOMEN'S HOUSEHOLD MONEY

In terms of evidence, to study money in the family is to enter largely uncharted territory. Although money is the major source of disagreements between husband and wife and often a sore point between parents and children, curiously, we know less about money matters than about family violence or even marital sex. Not only are families reluctant to disclose their private financial lives to strangers, but husbands, wives, and children often lie, deceive, or simply conceal information from each other as well. Perhaps more fundamental still, the model of what Amartya Sen calls the "glued-together family" has meant that questions about how money is divided among family members are seldom even asked. Once money enters the family, it is assumed to be somehow equitably distributed between family members, serving to maximize their collective welfare. How much money each person gets, how he or she obtains it, from whom and for what—these issues are rarely considered. And yet, as Michael Young suggested more than thirty years ago, the distribution of money among family members is often as lopsided and arbitrary as the distribution of national income among families. Therefore, Young argues, we should stop assuming that "some members of a family cannot be rich while others are poor." The period between 1870 and 1930 provides some unusual glimpses into this traditionally secret world of family money; at the turn of the century, as household finances became a contentious issue, the renegotiation of the domestic economy emerged from the usually closed doors of individual households to enter the public discourse.

How was a wife's money earmarked and set apart from other domestic monies? American women, even those whose husbands could afford it, never had a legal claim to any portion of domestic money. As long as spouses lived together, the author of a 1935 *Law Review* article explained, "the wife's right to support is not a right to any definite amount…Whether the wife will get much or little is not a matter of her legal right but is a matter for the husband to decide." The concept of a family wage—a salary that would support a male wage-earner and his dependent family—further increased married women's dependence on their husband's wages. As a result, the allocation of domestic money relied on unofficial rules and informal negotiation. At the turn of the century, married women—the majority of whom depended on their husbands' paychecks or incomes—obtained their cash through a variety of transfers.

Upper- and middle-class wives received an irregular dole or, more rarely, a regular allowance from their husbands for housekeeping expenses, including household goods and clothing. Sometimes women relied almost entirely on "invisible" dollars, crediting their expenses and rarely handling cash at all. Working-class wives, on the other hand, were given their husbands' paychecks and were expected to administer and distribute the family money. These official monies, however, were supervised and, even in the case of working-class women, ultimately owned and controlled by the husband. Sometimes, husbands openly took over all monetary transactions. In a letter to the advice column of the *Woman's Home Companion* in 1905, a thirty-year-old woman complained that John, her husband, although "liberal in a way… keeps the pocketbook himself, buys the provisions, prefers to purchase the dry-goods, the shoes, the gloves…and does not see that I need any money when he gets whatever I want." Even if a woman managed to save from her housekeeping expenses, the law ultimately considered that money to be her husband's property. For instance, in 1914, when Charles Montgomery sued his wife Emma for the $618.12 she had saved from the household expenses during their twenty-five years of marriage, Justice Blackman of the Brooklyn Supreme Court ruled for the husband, arguing "that no matter how careful and prudent has been the wife, if the money…belonged to the husband it is still his property, unless the evidence shows that it was a gift to his wife."

A wife's legitimate channels to additional cash were thus limited to a variety of persuasion techniques: asking, cajoling, or downright begging. And it was critical to master the rules of asking. Women were reminded that "to ask a tired, hungry man for anything is sheer waste of breath." The woman who "knows how," however, "wears her most becoming gown and puts his favorite dish before a man when she wants something." Sometimes only sexual blackmail worked. A mother of two children whose husband earned $250 a month but gave her only $75 for household expenses confided the secret of her "quick victory" to *Good Housekeeping:* "Last summer I knew I could never stand another year of absolute misery over money matters...On Monday night, after the best dinner I could serve, I told my husband...that unless he gave me $175 a month I would never let him so much as kiss me again...In the afternoon I had moved all my clothes...from our room to another across the hall." After a week of solitude he relented.

If such techniques of persuasion failed, there was also a repertoire of underground financial strategies, ranging from home pocket-picking to padding bills. In 1980, an article in the *Forum* denounced the "amount of deceit, fraud, and double dealing which grow out of the administration of the family finances." Just to obtain "a few dollars they can call their own," women routinely engaged in systematic domestic fraud; for example, some "get their milliners to send in a bill for forty dollars, instead of thirty, the real price, in order to take the extra ten to themselves...[others] overtax their tired eyes and exhausted bodies by taking in sewing without their husband's knowledge; and...farmer's wives...smuggled apples and eggs into town ..." In Elsa Herzfeld's study of families living in tenements on the West side of New York City in the early 1900s, wives disclosed some of their tricks; one woman told the investigator that while she knew her husband would "whip her" if he found out, she worked on "the sly," building a secret "store" under her mattress. Another wife "served" to earn some extra money, which she used to buy herself dresses for the "rackets." Sometimes, just to be able to send their parents some money, it appears that some immigrant women looked for ways of keeping their letters and money orders outside the home, hidden from their husbands.

Some methods were riskier: in 1905 Joseph Schultz was taken to the police court of Buffalo by Mrs. Schultz. It seems that Mr. Schultz, determined to stop his wife's nocturnal thefts of the change left in his trousers, set a small rattrap in the trouser pocket. At about 2:00 a.m. the trap was sprung, and next morning the husband was taken to court. *Bench and Bar*, a New York legal journal, reported with some satisfaction that the judge turned down the wife's complaint and upheld the right of husbands to maintain rattraps for the protection of their small change. In another case, Theresa Marabella, forty years old, was sentenced to four months in a county jail for stealing $10 from the trousers of Frank Marabella, a laborer from Bellport, New York, and her husband. She had spent the money on a trip to New York City.

But "stolen" dollars were not only taken by the wives of poor men. Indeed, one observer was persuaded that "the money skeletons in the closets of some nominally rich women may be as gruesome as are those in the closets of the nominally poor." While poor women rifled their husbands' trousers looking for some change, the affluent cashless wife used a variety of deceptive techniques. Mrs. Gray, a grandmother married for twenty years but without any money "she could call her own," was described as having "adopted a systematic policy of deceit and fraud toward her husband.... When she wants to give a little money to help buy a stove for a poor family, or to assist some sick or starving creature to pay his rent, she tells her husband that the flour is out, or that the sugar is low, and gets the needful amount." Thus this "strict church member" who never told a falsehood, paradoxically "cheats and deceives" the man "she has solemnly sworn to love and obey."

There were other ways to "circumvent the holder of the purse." Women bargained with dressmakers, milliners, and shopkeepers to add extra items in their bills so that, when the bill was paid, "the rich man's wife may get a rake-off and possess a few dollars." A Parisian-born New York dressmaker complained that American ladies got "costumes made and delivered that they wear one night and then return...they get $50 or $100 cash and have it charged as a dress or hats in the bill, so as to deceive their husbands." In search of cash, some women even turned to their servants, selling them their old furniture. A Japanese visitor to the United States in the second decade of the twentieth century was shocked to hear from "men and women of all classes, from newspapers, novels, lecturers, and once even from the pulpit... allusions to amusing stories of women secreting money in odd places, coaxing it from their husbands,...or saving it secretly for some private purpose."

The relative poverty of married women, however, grew increasingly untenable. How could a wife assume her added financial responsibilities as the household's "wage spender" if she had to ask, cajole, beg, or steal for her money and when so often she did not even know how much money was available to spend? The demand intensified for a more definite and regular housekeeping income for the wife and increasingly for her "private purse," a free sum of unaccounted money to spend for the home, entertainment, gifts, or on the many new consumer goods targeted at a female audience, such as clothes, cosmetics, or perfumes. As a forceful turn-of-the-century editorial in *Ladies' Home Journal* warned, the housewife was simply "not given the tools wherewith to work to the best advantage." While it was "all very well to go into spasms of indignation when one speaks of marriage as 'a business partnership,'" declared Edward Bok, the *Journal's* editor, marriage "must have a money basis," and domestic income should be treated as the "mutual affair" of husband and wife.

Think about how your family talks about money. Is it secretive? Open? Is it deceptive, as Zelizer notes about many families?

Zelizer's piece in this book is taken from a scholarly book in the field of sociology. Compare Zelizer's writing to Will's; do you find differences in tone or differences in the use of evidence? Given "A Dollar of Her Own," how would you characterize scholarly writing?

In a journal entry or blog post, imagine yourself in ten years with a career and spouse or domestic partner. What do you envision as the division of domestic labor and family finances? What are the benefits and problems of the arrangement you expect?

In a group, compare your ideas about gender and money. What differences do you find in your group? Zelizer notes that in late 19th and early 20th century America, there was a definite difference between men and women where money was concerned. Most 21st century Americans no longer have these kinds of ideas about money. Why do you suppose this is the case?

Mos Def, a Grammy and Emmy nominated musician and actor, comes from the socially conscious wing of Hip Hop, following in the footsteps of Public Enemy and KRS-One. "Got" appears on his third album, Black on Both Sides.

GOT

By Mos Def

Some cats really like to, you know,
profile and front.
And then the jooks go down, all at once they like,

Don't get me!
Don't get me!
Don't g-g-g-g-g-get me! (Repeat 3x)

You're out on the block hustling at the spot.
Got! This is how you get got.
At the gamblin' spot and your hand is mad hot.
Got! This is how you get got.
Out in Brooklyn late night flashing all of your rocks.
Got! This is how you get got.
Some girl from pink house said, "I like you a lot."
Got! This is how you get got.

This one goes to all them Big Will cats
with ice on they limbs and big rims on they Ac.
You rollin' around town with your system bump,
and your windows cracked low to profile and front.
Now, I like to have nice things just like you,

but I'm from Brooklyn, certain shit you just don't do,
like, high postin' when you far from home,
or like, high postin' when you all alone.
Now, this would seem to be clear common sense,
but cats be livin' off sheer confidence,
like "Fuck that, picture them tellin' me run that."
But acting invincible just ain't sensible.
It's nineteen ninety-now, and there's certain individuals
swear they rollin' hard and get robbed on principle.
Five-star general, flashin' on your revenue;
you takin' a ride on the downstate medical, like (whooooooo):
colorful sparks, yellow and blue,
a full-on attack and it's happening to you
with nothing you can do but bust back and cop a plea,
but five of them and one of you, that equals *Got* to me.

Don't get me.
Don't get me.
Don't g-g-g-g-g-get me. (Repeat 3x)

Come on, ya'll, now let's be real:
some jokers got a rough time keepin' it concealed.
I wonder what it mean: it's probably self-esteem;
They fiendin' to be seen, get hemmed like Gabardines.
Cats think it can't happen until the gats start clappin;
they comin' down the wire spittin' fire like a dragon
'Cause while the goods glisten, certain eyes take position
to observe your trick, and then catch that ass slippin'.
Like, come on now ock, what you expect?
Got a month's paycheck danglin' off your neck.
And while you Cristal sippin', they rubbin' up they mittens
with heat in mint condition to start the getti-gettin'.
They clique starts creepin' like Sandinista guerrillas.
You screamin' playa haters, these niggas is playa killers.
Mr. Fash—ion, that style never last long:
the harder you flash, the harder you get flashed on.
There's hunger in the street that is hard to defeat;

many steal for sport, but more steal to eat.
Cat's heavy at the weigh-in, and he's playin' for keeps.
Don't sleep, they'll roll up in your passenger's seat.
There is universal law, whether rich or poor,
some say life's a game, to more, life is war.
So put them egos to the side and get off them head-trips
'fore some cats pull out them heaters and make you head-less.

Don't get me.
Don't get me.
Don't g-g-g-g-g-get me. (Repeat 3x)

Going all the way back to "Rapper's Delight" by the Sugarhill Gang, many hip-hop artists have written songs about money or the good life. Find a number of songs that use this theme. What is the message of these songs, or what are the messages? Are money and material goods treated in different ways by different artists? Why do you suppose money is a popular motif in hip hop?

Analyze the message in "Got." What is Mos Def's attitude toward the display of expensive material goods? Write a journal entry or blog post discussing the message of the song while giving textual evidence from the lyrics.

Dan Ariely is a professor of Psychology and Behavioral Economics at Duke University. He is the author of two books: 2008's Predictably Irrational *and 2010's* The Upside of Irrationality, *from which this piece is excerpted. In* The Upside of Irrationality, *he performs experiments and relates historical episodes to point out that irrational decisions and faulty common wisdom occasionally have positive outcomes.*

excerpts from

PAYING MORE FOR LESS

By Dan Ariely

THE BONUS BONANZA

[...] In light of the financial crisis of 2008 and the subsequent outrage over the continuing bonuses paid to many of those deemed responsible for it, many people wonder how incentives really affect CEOs and Wall Street executives. Corporate boards generally assume that very large performance-based bonuses will motivate CEOs to invest more effort in their jobs and that the increased effort will result in higher quality output.[1] But is this really the case? Before you make up your mind, let's see what the empirical evidence shows.

To test the effectiveness of financial incentives as a device for enhancing performance, Nina Mazar (a professor at the University of Toronto), Uri Gneezy (a professor at the University of California at San Diego), George Loewenstein (a professor at Carnegie Mellon University), and I set up an experiment. We varied the amount of financial bonuses participants could receive if they performed well and measured the effect that the different incentive levels had on performance. In particular, we wanted to see whether

---

1 There have, of course, been many attempts to explain why it is rational to pay CEOs very high salaries, including one that I find particularly interesting but unlikely. According to this theory, executives get very high pay not because anyone thinks they earned it or deserve it but because paying them so much can motivate *other* people to work hard in the hope that they too will one day be overpaid like the CEO. The funny thing about this theory is that if you follow it to its logical conclusion, you would not only pay CEOs ridiculously high salaries, but you would also force them to spend more time with their friends and families and send them on expensive vacations in order to complete the picture of a perfect life—because this would be the best way to motivate other people to try to become CEOs.

offering very large bonuses would increase performance, as we usually expect, or decrease performance [...]

[...] Before I tell you the results, how well do you think the participants in the three groups did? Would you guess that those who could earn a medium-level bonus did better than those who were faced with the small one? Do you think those hoping for a very large bonus did better than those who could achieve a medium-level one? We found that those who could earn a small bonus (equivalent to one day of pay) and the medium-level bonus (equivalent to two weeks' worth of work) did not differ much from each other. We concluded that since even our small payment was worth a substantial amount to our participants, it probably already maximized their motivation. But how did they perform when the very large bonus (the amount equivalent to five months of their regular pay rate) was on the line? As you can tell from the figure, the data from our experiment showed that people, at least in this regard, are very much like rats. Thos who stood to earn the most demonstrated the lowest level of performance. Relative to those in the low-or-medium-bonus conditions, they achieved good or very good performance less than a third of the time. The experience was so stressful to those in the very-large-bonus condition that they choked under the pressure, much like the rats in the Yerkes and Dodson experiment.

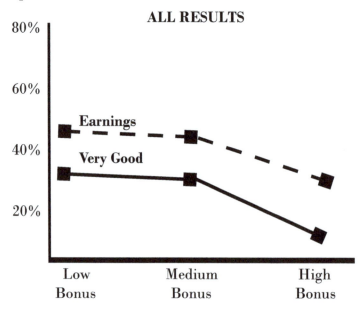

ALL RESULTS

The graph summarizes the results for the three bonus conditions across the six games. The "very good" line represents the percentage of people in each condition who achieved this level of performance. The "earnings" line represents the percentage of total payoff that people in each condition earned.

[...] What did this experiment teach us? As you might expect, we saw a difference between the effects of large incentives on the two types of tasks. When the job at hand involved only clicking two keys on a keyboard, higher bonuses led to higher performance. However, once the task required even some rudimentary cognitive skills (in the form of simple math problems), the higher incentives led to a negative effect on performance, just as we had seen in the experiment in India.

The conclusion was clear: Paying people high bonuses can result in high performance when it comes to simple mechanical tasks, but the opposite can happen when you ask them to use their brains—which is usually what companies try to do when they pay executives very high bonuses. If senior vice presidents were paid to lay bricks, motivating them through high bonuses would make sense. But people who receive bonus-based incentives for thinking about mergers and acquisitions or coming up with complicated financial instruments could be far less effective than we tend to think—and there may even be negative consequences to really large bonuses.

To summarize, using money to motivate people can be a double-edged sword. For tasks that require cognitive ability, low to moderate performance-based incentives can help. But when the incentive level is very high, it can command too much attention and thereby distract the person's mind with thoughts about the reward. This can create stress and ultimately reduce the level of performance [...]

[...] WHAT ABOUT THOSE "SPECIAL PEOPLE"?

A few years ago, before the financial crisis of 2008, I was invited to give a talk to a select group of bankers. The meeting took place in a well-appointed conference room at a large investment company's office in New York City. The food and wine were delicious and the views from the windows spectacular. I told the audience about different projects I was working on, including the experiments on high bonuses in India and MIT. They all nodded their heads in agreement with the theory that high bonuses might backfire—until I suggested that the same psychological effects might also apply to the people in the room. They were clearly offended by the suggestion. The idea that their bonuses could negatively influence their work performance was preposterous, they claimed.

I tried another approach and asked for a volunteer from the audience to describe how the work atmosphere at his firm changes at the end of the year. "During November and December," the fellow said, "very little work gets done. People mostly think about their bonuses and about what they will be able to afford." In response, I asked the audience to try on the idea that the focus on their upcoming bonuses might have a negative effect on their performance, but they refused to see my point. Maybe it was the alcohol, but I suspect that those folks simply didn't want to acknowledge the possibility that their bonuses were vastly oversized. (As the prolific author and journalist Upton Sinclair once noted, "It is difficult to get a man to understand something when his salary depends upon his not understanding it.")

Somewhat unsurprisingly, when presented with the results of these experiments, the bankers also maintained that they were, apparently, superspecial individuals; unlike most people, they insisted, they work better under stress. It didn't seem to me that they were really so different from other people, but I conceded that perhaps they were right. I invited them to come to the lab so that we could run an experiment to find out for sure. But, given how busy bankers are and the size of their paychecks, it was impossible to tempt them to take part in our experiments or to offer them a bonus that would have been large enough to be meaningful for them.

Without the ability to test bankers, Racheli Barkan (a professor at Ben-Gurion University in Israel) and I looked for another source of data that could help us understand how highly paid, highly specialized professionals perform under great pressure. I know nothing about basketball, but Racheli is an expert, and she suggested that we look at clutch players—the basketball heroes who sink a basket just as the buzzer sounds. Clutch players are paid much more than other players, and are presumed to perform especially brilliantly during the last few minutes or seconds of a game, when stress and pressure are highest.

With the help of Duke University men's basketball Coach Mike Krzyzewski ("Coach K"), we got a group of professional coaches to identify clutch players in the NBA (the coaches agreed, to a large extent about who is and who is not a clutch player). Next, we watched videos of the twenty most crucial games for each clutch player in an entire NBA season (by most crucial, we meant that the score difference at the end of the game did not exceed three points). For each of those games, we measured how many points the clutch players had shot in the last five minutes of the first half of each game, when pressure was relatively low. Then we compared that number to the number of points scored during the last five minutes of the game, when the outcome was hanging by a thread and stress was at its peak. We also noted the same measures for all the other "nonclutch" players who were playing in the same games.

We found that the nonclutch players scored more or less the same in the low-stress and high-stress moments, whereas there was actually a substantial improvement for clutch players during the last five minutes of the games. So far it looked good for the clutch players and, by analogy, the bankers, as it seemed that some highly qualified people could, in fact, perform better under pressure.

But—and I'm sure you expected a "but"—there are two ways to gain more points in the last five minutes of the game. An NBA clutch player can either improve his percentage success (which would indicate a sharpening of performance) or shoot more often with the same percentage (which suggests no improvement in skill but rather a change in the number of attempts). So we looked separately at whether the clutch players actually shot better or just more often. As it turned out, the clutch players did not improve their skill; they just tried many more times. Their field goal percentage did not increase in the last five minutes (meaning that their shots were no more accurate); neither was it the case that nonclutch players got worse.

At this point you probably think that clutch players are guarded more heavily during the end of the game and this is why they don't show the expected increase in performance. To see if this were indeed the case, we counted how many times they were fouled and also looked at their free throws. We found the same pattern: The heavily guarded clutch players were fouled more and got to shoot from the free-throw line more frequently, but their scoring percentage was unchanged. Certainly, clutch players are very good players, but our analysis showed that, contrary to common belief, their performance doesn't improve in the last, most important part of the game.

Obviously, NBA players are not bankers. The NBA is much more selective than the financial industry; very few people are sufficiently skilled to play professional basketball, while many, many people work as professional bankers. As we've seen, it's also easier to get positive returns from high incentives when we're talking about physical rather than cognitive skills. NBA players use both, but playing basketball is more of a physical than a mental activity (at least relative to banking). So it would be far more challenging for the bankers to demonstrate "clutch" abilities when the task is less physical and demands more gray matter. Also, since the basketball players don't actually improve under pressure, it's even more unlikely that bankers would be able to perform to a higher degree when they are under the gun. [...]

The documentary film *Inside Job* and numerous other sources exposed the biggest banks in the country for giving billions of dollars in executive bonuses, even immediately before, during, and after the financial crisis that began in September, 2008. Using reputable internet sources or news magazines, give yourself a concrete sense of the high bonuses that Ariely is talking about in this excerpt: how big is big? What multiple of the cost of your four-year education did an executive at Goldman-Sachs get as a bonus in 2009?

In your life, how is motivation linked to money? Consider the things that you're motivated to do—maybe work, school, hobbies, or sports. What motivates you? Does money enter into the equation? Would more money increase your motivation to do a good job?

Jaron Lanier, one of the pioneers of virtual reality research in the 1980s, is a scientist-philospher named, in 2010, by TIME magazine as one of the 100 most influential people in the world. He is a programmer, writer, musician, and artist. His 2010 book, You Are Not a Gadget, *from which this reading is excerpted, argues that the demonetization of creative work (music, journalism, and film) has serious consequences for our culture.*

excerpts from

YOU ARE NOT A GADGET

By Jaron Lanier

THE CITY IS BUILT TO MUSIC

The fates of musicians in the emerging digital economy are examined.

HOW LONG IS TOO LONG TO WAIT?

A little over a decade and a half ago, with the birth of the World Wide Web, a clock started. The old-media empires were put on a path of predictable obsolescence. But would a superior replacement arise in time? What idealists said then was, "Just wait! More opportunities will be created than destroyed." Isn't fifteen years long enough to wait before we switch from hope to empiricism? The time has come to ask, "Are we building the digital utopia for people or machines?" If it's people, we have a problem.

Open culture revels in bizarre, exaggerated perceptions of the evils of the record companies or anyone else who thinks there was some merit in the old models of intellectual property. For many college students, sharing files is considered an act of civil disobedience. That would mean that stealing digital material puts you in the company of Gandhi and Martin Luther King![1]

1 For an example of this common rationalization, here's a quote from an essay by "Sharkhead007" found on the site Big Nerds, which describes itself as a "free essay and coursework database" (meaning students use it to avoid writing assignments): "Critics would say that...if the government says something is illegal, it is morally wrong to go against it. However, Henry David Thoreau wrote a famous essay called Civil Disobedience, which described that sometimes the public has to revolt against law... Public activists and leaders such as Gandhi and Martin Luther King Jr. adopted the ideas expressed in Thoreau's essay and used them to better the lives of the people they were fighting for. Download-

It's true that the record companies have not helped themselves. They have made a public fuss about suing the most sympathetic people, snooped obnoxiously, and so on. Furthermore, there's a long history of sleaze, corruption, creative accounting, and price fixing in the music business.

> If we choose to pry culture away from capitalism while the rest of life is still capitalistic, culture will become a slum. In fact, online culture increasingly resembles a slum in disturbing ways. Slums have more advertising than wealthy neighborhoods, for instance. People are meaner in slums; mob rule and vigilantism are commonplace. If there is a trace of "slumming" in the way that many privileged young people embrace current online culture, it is perhaps an echo of 1960s counterculture.

DREAMS STILL DIE HARD

By 2008, some of the leading lights of the open culture movement started to acknowledge the obvious, which is that not everyone has benefited from the movement. A decade ago we all assumed, or at least hoped, that the net would bring so many benefits to so many people that those unfortunates who weren't being paid for what they used to do would end up doing even better by finding new ways to get paid. You still hear that argument being made, as if people lived forever and can afford to wait an eternity to have the new source of wealth revealed to them.

Kevin Kelly wrote in 2008 that the new utopia:

> *is famously good news for two classes of people: a few lucky aggregators, such as Amazon and Netflix, and 6 billion consumers. Of those two, I think consumers earn the greater reward from the wealth hidden in infinite niches.*

> *But the long tail is a decidedly mixed blessing for creators. Individual artists, producers, inventors and makers are overlooked in the equation. The long tail does not raise the sales of creators much, but it does add massive competition and endless downward pressure on prices. Unless*

---

ing music from the Internet, although it may not be as profound as freeing people from bondage and persecution, is a form of civil disobedience. It is a revolt against a corrupt system put in place for the sole purpose of making money, regardless of the welfare of the consumer or the artist."

artists become a large aggregator of other artists' works, the long tail offers no path out of the quiet doldrums of minuscule sales.

The people who devote their lives to making committed cultural expression that can be delivered through the cloud—as opposed to casual contributions that require virtually no commitment—well, those people are, Kevin acknowledges, the losers.

His new advice at the time was similar to the sorts of things we used to suggest in fits of anticipation and wild hope ten, fifteen, and even twenty-five years ago. He suggested that artists, musicians, or writers find something that isn't digital related to their work, such as live appearances, T-shirt sales, and so on, and convince a thousand people to spend $100 each per year for whatever that is. Then an artist could earn $100,000 a year.

I very much want to believe that this can be done by more than a tiny number of people who happen to benefit from unusual circumstances. The occasional dominatrix or life coach can use the Internet to implement this plan. But after ten years of seeing many, many people try, I fear that it won't work for the vast majority of journalists, musicians, artists, and filmmakers who are staring into career oblivion because of our failed digital idealism.

My skepticism didn't come easily. Initially I assumed that entrepreneurial fervor and ingenuity would find a way. As part of researching this book, I set out once again to find some cultural types who were benefiting from open culture.

THE SEARCH

We have a baseline in the form of the musical middle class that is being put out of business by the net. We ought to at least find support in the new economy for them. Can 26,000 musicians each find 1,000 true fans? Or can 130,000 each find between 200 and 600 true fans? Furthermore, how long would be too long to wait for this to come about? Thirty years? Three hundred years? Is there anything wrong with enduring a few lost generations of musicians while we wait for the new solution to emerge?

The usual pattern one would expect is an S curve: There would be only a small number of early adaptors, but a noticeable trend of increase in their numbers. It is common in Silicon Valley to see incredibly fast adoption of new behaviors.

There were only a few pioneer bloggers for a little while—then, suddenly, there were millions of them. The same could happen for musicians making a living in the new economy.

So at this point in time, a decade and a half after the start of the web, a decade after the widespread adoption of music file sharing, how many examples of musicians living by new rules should we expect to find?

Just to pick a rough number out of the air, it would be nice if there were 3,000 by now. Then maybe in a few years there would be 30,000. Then the S curve would manifest in full, and there would be 300,000. A new kind of professional musician ought to thunder onto the scene with the shocking speed of a new social networking website.

Based on the rhetoric about how much opportunity there is out there, you might think that looking for 3,000 is cynical. There must be tens of thousands already! Or you might be a realist, and think that it's still early; 300 might be a more realistic figure.

I was a little afraid to just post about my quest openly on the net, because even though I'm a critic of the open/free orthodoxy I didn't want to jinx it if it had a chance. Suppose I came up with a desultory result? Would that discourage people who would otherwise have made the push to make the new economy work?

Kevin Kelly thought my fear was ridiculous. He's more of a technological determinist: He thinks the technology will find a way to achieve its destiny whatever people think. So he volunteered to publicize my quest on his popular technium blog in the expectation that exemplars of the new musical economy would come forward.

I also published a fire-breathing opinion piece in the *New York Times* and wrote about my fears in other visible places, all in the hope of inspiring contact from the new vanguard of musicians who are making a living off the open web.

In the old days—when I myself was signed to a label—there were a few major artists who made it on their own, like Ani DiFranco. She became a *millionaire* by selling her own CDs when they were still a high-margin product people were used to buying, back before the era of file sharing. Has a new army of Ani DiFrancos started to appear?

THE CASE OF THE MISSING BENEFICIARIES

To my shock, I have had trouble finding even a handful of musicians who can be said to be following in DiFranco's footsteps. Quite a few musicians contacted me to claim victory in the new order, but again and again, they turned out to not be the real thing.

Here are some examples of careers that *do* exist but do not fill me with hope for the future:

- **The giant musical act from the old days of the record business, grabbing a few headlines by posting music for free downloading:** Radiohead is an example. I want to live in a world where new musicians can potentially succeed to the degree Radiohead has succeeded, but under a new order, not the old order. Where are they?

- **The aggregator:** A handful of musicians run websites that aggregate the music of hundreds or thousands of others. There are a few services that offer themed streaming music, for instance. One is a specialized new age music website that serves some paying yoga studios. The aggregator in this case is not Google, so only a trickle of money is made. The aggregated musicians make essentially nothing. Very few people can be aggregators, so this career path will not "scale," as we say in Silicon Valley.

- **The jingle/sound track/TV composor:** You can still make money from getting music placed in a setting that hasn't been destroyed by file sharing yet. Some examples are movie and TV sound tracks, commercial jingles, and so on. You can use internet presence to promote this kind of career. The problem with this strategy in the long term is that these paying options are themselves under siege.

- **The vanity career:** This is a devilish one. Music is glamorous, so there are perhaps more people who claim to be making a living as musicians than are actually doing so. There have probably always been way more people who have tried to have a music career than have succeeded at it. This is massively true online. There are hundreds of thousands of musicians seeking exposure on sites like MySpace, Bebo, YouTube, and on and on, and it is absolutely clear that most of them are not making a living from being there.

There is a seemingly limitless supply of people who want to pretend that they have professional music careers and will pay flacks to try to create the illusion. I am certainly not a private detective, but it takes only a few casual web searches to discover that a particular musician inherited a fortune and is barely referenced outside of his own website.

- **Kids in a van:** If you are young and childless, you can run around in a van to gigs, and you can promote those gigs online. You will make barely any money, but you can crash on couches and dine with fans you meet through the web. This is a good era for that kind of musical adventure. If I were in my twenties I would be doing it. But it is a youthiness career. Very few people can raise kids with that lifestyle. It's treacherous in the long run, as youth fades.

One example of success brought up again and again is Jonathan Coulton. He has a nice career centered on spoofs and comedy songs, and his audience is the geeky crowd. He is certainly not becoming a millionaire, but at least he seems to have authentically reached the level of being able to reliably support a family without the assistance of the old-media model (though he does have a Hollywood agent, so he isn't an example to please the purist). There were only a handful of other candidates. The comedy blogger Ze Frank occasionally recorded tunes on his site, for example, and made money from a liquor ad placed there.

The tiny number of success stories is worrisome. The history of the web is filled with novelty-driven success stories that can never be repeated. One young woman started a website simply asking for donations to help her pay down her credit cards, and it worked! But none of the many people who tried to replicate her trick met with success.

This is astonishing to me. By now, a decade and a half into the web era, when iTunes has become the biggest music store, in a period when companies like Google are the beacons of Wall Street, shouldn't there at least be a few thousand initial pioneers of a new kind of musical career who can survive in our utopia? Maybe more will appear soon, but the current situation is discouraging.

Up-and-coming musicians in the open world can increasingly choose between only two options: they can try to follow the trail of mouse clicks laid down by Jonathan Coulton (and apparently almost no one can do that) or they can seek more reliable sustenance, by becoming refugees within the last dwindling pockets of the old-media world they were just assaulting a moment before.

Of course, eventually the situation might become transformed into something better. Maybe after a generation or two without professional musicians, some new habitat will emerge that will bring them back.

> The people who are perhaps the most screwed by open culture are the middle classes of intellectual and cultural creation. The freelance studio session musician faces diminished prospects, for instance. Another example, outside of the world of music, is the stringer selling reports to newspapers from a war zone. These are both crucial contributors to culture and democracy. Each pays painful dues and devotes years to honing a craft. They used to live off the trickle-down effects of the old system, and, like the middle class at large, they are precious. They get nothing from the new system.

THE LORDS OF THE CLOUDS RENOUNCE FREE WILL
IN ORDER TO BECOME INFINITELY LUCKY

Out-of-control financial instruments are linked to the fates of musicians and the fallacies of cybernetic totalism.

REGIONAL FATES

China's precipitous climb into wealth has been largely based on cheap, high-quality labor. But the real possibility exists that sometime in the next two decades a vast number of jobs in China and elsewhere will be made obsolete by advances in cheap robotics so quickly that it will be a cruel shock to hundreds of millions of people.

If waves of technological change bring new kinds of employment with them, what will it be like? Thus far, all computer-related technologies built by humans are endlessly confusing, buggy, tangled, fussy, and error-ridden. As a result, the icon of employment in the age of information has been the help desk.

For many years I've proposed that the "help desk," defined nobly and broadly to include such things as knowledge management, data forensics, software consulting, and so on, can provide us with a way to imagine a world in which capitalism and advanced technology can coexist with a fully employed population of human beings. This is a scenario I call "Planet of the Help Desks."

This brings us to India. India's economy has been soaring at the same time as China's, much to the amazement of observers everywhere, but on a model that is significantly different from China's. As Esther Dyson has pointed out, the Indian economy excels in "nonroutine" services.

India, thanks to its citizens' facility with English, hosts a huge chunk of the world's call centers, as well as a significant amount of software development, creative production like computer animation, outsourced administrative services, and increasingly, health care.

AMERICA IN DREAMLAND

Meanwhile, the United States has chosen a different path entirely. While there is a lot of talk about networks and emergence from the top American capitalists and technologists, in truth most of them are hoping to thrive by controlling the network that everyone else is forced to pass through.

Everyone wants to be a lord of a computing cloud. For instance, James Surowiecki in *The Wisdom of Crowds* extols an example in which an online crowd helped find gold in a gold mine even though the crowd didn't own the gold mine.

There are many forms of this style of yearning. The United States still has top universities and corporate labs, so we'd like the world to continue to accept intellectual property laws that send money our way based on our ideas, even when those ideas are acted on by others. We'd like to indefinitely run the world's search engines, computing clouds, advertising placement services, and social networks, even as our old friend/demon Moore's law makes it possible for new competitors to suddenly appear with ever greater speed and thrift.

We'd like to channel the world's finances through our currency to the benefit of our hedge fund schemes. Some of us would like the world to pay to watch our action movies and listen to our rock music into the indefinite future, even though others of us have been promoting free media services in order to own the cloud that places ads. Both camps are hoping that one way or another they will own the central nodes of the network even as they undermine each other.

Once again, this is an oversimplification. There are American factories and help desks. But, to mash up metaphors, can America maintain a virtual luxury yacht floating on the sea of the networks of the world? Or will our central tollbooth on all smart things sink under its own weight into an ocean of global connections? Even if we can win at the game, not many Americans will be employed keeping our yacht afloat, because it looks as though India will continue to get better at running help desks.

I'll be an optimist and suggest that America will somehow convince the world to allow us to maintain our privileged role. The admittedly flimsy reasons are that a) we've done it before, so they're used to us, and b) the alternatives are potentially less appealing to many global players, so there might be widespread grudging acceptance of at least some kinds of long-term American centrality as a least-bad option.

COMPUTATIONALLY ENHANCED CORRUPTION

Corruption has always been possible without computers, but computers have made it easier for criminals to pretend even to themselves that they are not aware of their own schemes. The savings and loan scandals of the 1980s were possible without extensive computer network services. All that was required was a misuse of a government safety net. More recent examples of cataclysmic financial mismanagement, starting with Enron and Long-Term Capital Management, could have been possible only with the use of big computer networks. The wave of financial calamities that took place in 2008 were significantly cloud based.

No one in the pre-digital cloud era had the mental capacity to lie to him or herself in the way we routinely are able to now. The limitations of organic human memory and calculation used to put a cap on the intricacies of self delusion. In finance, the rise of computer-assisted hedge funds and similar operations has turned capitalism into a search engine. You tend the engine in the computing cloud, and it searches for money. It's analogous to someone showing up in a casino with a supercomputer and a bunch of fancy sensors. You can certainly win at gambling with high-tech help, but to do so you must supercede the game you are pretending to play. The casino will object, and in the case of investment in the real world, society should also object.

Visiting the offices of financial cloud engines (like high-tech hedge funds) feels like visiting the Googleplex. There are software engineers all around, but few of the sorts of topical experts and analysts who usually populate investment houses. These pioneers have brought capitalism into a new phase, and I don't think it's working.

In the past, an investor had to be able to understand at least something about what an investment would actually accomplish. Maybe a building would be built, or a product would be shipped somewhere, for instance. No more. There are so many layers of abstraction between the new kind of elite investor and actual events on the ground that the investor no longer has any concept of what is actually being done as a result of investments.

THE CLOUDY EDGE BETWEEN SELF-DELUSION AND CORRUPTION

True believers in the hive mind seem to think that no number of layers of abstraction in a financial system can dull the efficacy of the system. According to the new ideology, which is blending a cyber cloud faith and neo-Milton Friedman economics, the market will not only do what's best, it will do better the less people understand it. I disagree. The financial crisis brought about by the U.S. mortgage meltdown of 2008 was a case of too many people believing in the cloud too much.

Each layer of digital abstraction, no matter how well it is crafted, contributes some degree of error and obfuscation. No abstraction corresponds to reality perfectly. A lot of such layers become a system unto themselves, one that functions apart from the reality that is obscured far below. Making money in the cloud doesn't necessarily bring rain to the ground.

THE BIG *N*

Here we come to one way that the ideal of "free" music and the corruption of the financial world are connected.

Silicon Valley has actively proselytized Wall Street to buy into the doctrines of open/free culture and crowdsourcing. According to Chris Anderson, for instance, Bear Stearns issued a report in 2007 "to address *pushback* and other objections from media industry heavyweights who make up a big part of Bear Stearns's client base."

What the heavyweights were pushing back against was the Silicon Valley assertion that "content" from identifiable humans would no longer matter, and that the chattering of the crowd with itself was a better business bet than paying people to make movies, books, and music.

Chris identified his favorite quote from the Bear Stearns report:

> *For as long as most can recall, the entertainment industry has lived by the axiom "content is king." However, no one company has proven consistently capable of producing "great content," as evidenced by volatility in TV ratings and box office per film for movie studios, given the inherent fickleness of consumer demand for entertainment goods.*

As Chris explains, "despite the bluster about track records and taste…it's all a crapshoot. Better to play the big-*n* statistical game of User Generated Content, as YouTube has, than place big bets on a few horses like network TV."

"Big-*n*" refers to "*n*," a typical symbol for a mathematical variable. If you have a giant social network, like Facebook, perhaps some variable called *n* gains big value. As *n* gets larger, statistics become more reliable. This might also mean, for example, that it becomes more likely that someone in the crowd will happen to provide you with a free gem of a song or video.

However, it must be pointed out that in practice, even if you believe in the big *n* as a substitute for judgment, *n* is almost never big enough to mean anything on the internet. As vast as the internet has become, it usually isn't vast enough to generate valid statistics. The overwhelming majority of entries garnering reviews on sites like Yelp or Amazon have far too few reviewers to reach any meaningful level of statistical utility. Even when *n* is large, there's no guarantee it's valid.

In the old order, there were occasional smirks and groans elicited by egregious cases of incompetence. Such affronts were treated as exceptions to the rule. In general it was assumed that the studio head, the hedge fund manager, and the CEO actually did have some special skills, some reason to be in a position of great responsibility.

In the new order, there is no such presumption. The crowd works for free, and statistical algorithms supposedly take the risk out of making bets if you are a lord of the cloud. Without risk, there is no need for skill. But who is that lord who owns the cloud that connects the crowd? Not just anybody. A lucky few (for luck is all that can possibly be involved) will own it. Entitlement has achieved its singularity and become infinite.

Unless the algorithm actually isn't perfect. But we're rich enough that we can delay finding out if it's perfect or not. This is the grand unified scam of the new ideology.

It should be clear that the madness that has infected Wall Street is just another aspect of the madness that insists that if music *can* be delivered for free, it *must* be delivered for free. The Facebook Kid and the Cloud Lord are serf and king of the new order.

In each case, human creativity and understanding, especially one's own creativity and understanding, are treated as worthless. Instead, one trusts in the crowd, in the big n, in the algorithms that remove the risks of creativity in ways too sophisticated for any mere person to understand.

Lanier draws a parallel between online culture and slums (page 126), seeing similarities in the landscapes, the systems of order, and the behaviors of the citizenry. Consider the physical environments in which you have lived: What do they look like? How do individuals maintain their safety, their sense of space, their privacy, or their attitudes? Now, contrast those places with the technological environments in which you spend time. How are people's expectations different? Their behaviors? Their desires? Their codes of ethics? Describe what eBay, Facebook, YouTube, or another website might look like if it occupied physical space. Would it feel safe, fun, overwhelming, lawless, or something else?

In your own mind, how does the online environment seem to change the value of a physical thing by rendering it electronic? Consider how much you can get for free online through illegitimate, illegal, or unauthorized sources. For example, software, music, images, artwork, and schoolwork. Do you feel the same way toward these digital items as you do toward physical objects? What is the difference between downloading a few mp3s and swiping a CD from a record store?

Many of you, statistics would suggest, may have illegally downloaded music. In a small group, discuss this behavior in the context of Lanier's argument about professional musicianship in the digital age. Ignoring for the moment the question of ethicality, think about the economic implications of enjoying "free" music, particularly that made by up-and-coming artists trying to ply their trade in the modern world. Do you believe, as Lanier says some still do, that a solution will eventually come from the market? Do you agree with the essay writer he quotes on page 125 that music pirating is "civil disobedience" akin to that advocated by Thoreau? Or, do you think something else needs to happen to maintain the place of the professional artist in Western culture? Under what conditions should artists be paid for their work, and when should that system of remuneration be governed or protected?

Julian Dibbell is a technology journalist who writes about online culture. His 2006 book, Play Money: or, How I Quit My Day Job and Made Millions Trading Virtual Loot, *describes his experiences selling virtual items to players of MMORPGs (massively multi-player online roleplaying games). He has appeared in* The Best Technology Writing *series and edited the 2010 edition. This article about former child actor Brock Pierce appeared in* Wired *magazine in 2008.*

excerpts from

THE DECLINE AND FALL OF AN ULTRA RICH ONLINE GAMING EMPIRE

By Julian Dibbell

For a long time, maybe a year and a half, the game was pretty much what remained of Brock Pierce's life: He would wake up, sit down at his computer, log in, and play. Thirteen dollars a month bought him around-the-clock access to this imaginary world, a place of perilous dungeons and enchanted woods where online gamers came together by the thousands in a never-ending quest for treasure. Some assumed the roles of dwarves or lizard-people; some were humans. Pierce would play for hours—as long as 24 hours without a break—slaying monsters, wresting precious coins and jewels and magic weapons from their corpses. Later, he added extra computers to his setup and taught himself to play as many as six characters at once, one per machine. After that he'd sit there in the glow of half a dozen monitors, hands flitting from keyboard to keyboard, eyes shifting from screen to screen, yet still, somehow, not finding time enough for all there was to accomplish in the game.

"There were times I came outside," he says, "and the sun hurt."

Pierce was 19 at the time and hardly the first young American male to step away from the sometimes painful light of reality for an extended, free-falling obsession with an online fantasy videogame. But it's safe to say that the reality he was shrinking from in 2000 was not that of a typical teen. At 16, Pierce had retired from a career as a modestly successful Hollywood child actor; by 18,

s a dazzlingly successful dotcom entrepreneur, living large on a $250,000
utive salary and the promise of millions more in post-IPO equity. By his
h birthday he had lost it all. Pierce's high-profile startup had flamed out in
blaze of scandal that included accusations of sex with minors, and he and
his cofounders had found it prudent to leave the U.S. He lived now in a rented
house in a strange country, on the dwindling remains of a crash-ravaged stock
portfolio.

And he played the game. You could call it solace: A way to fill the emptiness
of failure with the curiously convincing sense of purpose that comes from
steadily amassing a make-believe digital fortune in magic staves and platinum
coins. But in time it would be more than that. Much more. Soon enough, amid
the daily grind of his obsession, he would see in the game itself a way out of
the bleak hole he had fallen into. He would take a clear-eyed, calculating look
at what he and his fellow players had been doing all those months—at the
countless hours they'd given over to the pursuit of purely virtual but implacably
scarce commodities—and he would recognize it not just for the underexploited
form of productivity it was but for the highly profitable commercial enterprise
it might sustain. He would spend the next half decade bringing that business
to life. And though some people would hate what he was building, and others
would want to take it all away from him, there would come a day when Pierce,
eight years older, could look back on an accomplishment that was bigger than
he had ever envisioned—and stranger than he would ever comprehend.

That day has come, and it's a Saturday: A bright, clean Saturday in the
hills above Los Angeles, where the views from Pierce's $3 million house are
impressive. From the poolside patio, you can look down across West Hollywood
and Beverly Hills all the way to the rolling breakers off Santa Monica. In the
living room, big canvasses by high-end contemporary LA artists hang on the
walls. The views are also impressive in the kitchen, where a row of empty wine
bottles includes a $5,000 1945 Domaine de la Romanée-Conti.

That Pierce lives the life of a former corporate mogul at the age of 28 is
remarkable enough in itself. Even more so, perhaps, is that he got here by
dominating an industry in which orcs, trolls, elves, dwarves, and minotaurs are
major segments of both the customer base and the labor force. That industry
is known to insiders as real-money trading, or RMT, and if I tell you now that
I've made some money in it myself, that's not because I expect you to take it
on my say-so that there are people who might pay as much as $1,800 for an

eight-piece suit of Skyshatter chain mail made entirely of fiction and code. Or that there are millions more—players of *World of Warcraft*, *Age of Conan*, *EverQuest*, *EVE Online*, and other massively multiplayer online role-playing games (MMORPGs, or MMOs)—who have given other players real money in exchange for the virtual weapons, armor, currencies, and other sought-after items around which these games revolve. Or that despite the game companies' widespread prohibition of such transactions, their number has grown to support an estimated $2 billion annual trade, a half dozen multimillion-dollar online retail businesses, and an enormous Chinese workforce earning 30 cents an hour playing MMOs and harvesting treasure to supply the major retailers.

It's all true, but don't take my word for it: Just ask any of the world's 20 million MMO gamers, for whom real-money trading has become commonplace, despised by some as a form of cheating and a blight on play, accepted by others as a necessary shortcut through some of the most elaborate (and time-consuming) games ever made. I'm mentioning my own familiarity with RMT—I spent most of 2003 peddling virtual items on eBay and made, if you must know, a grand total of $11,356.70—only to establish that I was around before the virtual treasure trade got to be big business.

Which is to say, I was around before Brock Pierce and the company he founded—Internet Gaming Entertainment—made its mark on the industry. I was around before most people in the trade had even heard of IGE, let alone before it became a synonym for virtual currency sales. I was around when RMT as a profession was almost exclusively the province of small-timers like me and the very notion of a multinational, 500-employee virtual-items business doing over a quarter billion dollars in trades was practically unimaginable. And I was around three years later when rumors of a $60 million Goldman Sachs investment in IGE first broke and for a moment it seemed possible that Pierce had a handle on something deeper and more enduring than just a profitable business: The future maybe, not only of virtual retailing but of economic life in general.

And I am here today, admiring the views at Pierce's LA home, because I figure it's my best shot at an answer to the only question I can think of asking in the face of a story like IGE's: How did it happen?

Pierce, standing in his kitchen, considers the question for a moment and dives in, going all the way back to when he first learned there might be more to videogames than pure amusement: "Avid gamer my whole life, from a very young age," he says. "I played *Mortal Kombat* competitively in arcades. Played for money at 10, hustling the 20-year-olds. Five bucks on whoever wins. Which, at 10 years old, is real money."

He smiles as he talks, and it's a smile I've seen before. You may have, too, actually: Right there in your local Blockbuster on the cover of the 1996 Disney romp *First Kid*, in which a 15-year-old Pierce starred opposite the immortal Sinbad. His appearance hasn't changed much—he has the doe-eyed good looks and elfin dimensions of an eternal golden boy—but it's the smile that has changed the least. Relaxed and open and at the same time taut with the intention to appear relaxed and open, it's an actor's smile, a mask. And it occurs to me that if I'm ever going to get through to what's behind it, this story is going to have to begin somewhere else. [...]

[...] He moved on to the world of business, more specifically to the world of Collins-Rector and Shackley, which by all accounts was a lively one. They'd recently bought a $2.5 million mansion in Encino, California. Studded with waterfalls and aquariums and equipped with a swimming pool, a screening room, and a hot tub for 12, the sprawling M&C Estate (for "Marc & Chad") was made for parties and reportedly saw its share. Pierce became a fixture at the place, but ultimately his presence there was not about the parties. It was about the future that Collins-Rector and Shackley seemed to be offering when they invited him to join them as a founder of DEN.

Pierce says he has no regrets about taking them up on it. "DEN was an incredible opportunity to learn," he says. "That was business school." But frankly, it was not the sort of b-school anybody wants to have on their rèsumè. DEN indeed took off, and over the three years of its existence it went on gathering momentum, soaking up nearly $90 million in venture funds before self-destructing and becoming what it remains: A canonical example of dotcom-era excess and absurdity. [...]

[...] By the time DEN finally laid off its last employees in May 2000, the founders were living quietly in Spain, in the seaside resort town of Marbella. Pierce, however, was spending most of his time in another place altogether:

the magical universe of Norrath, in which *EverQuest* (then the Western world's biggest MMO) took place.

The relative appeal of Norrath wasn't hard to explain. Spain was nice enough, but it was still undeniably part of the same real world in which Pierce's fortunes had lately gone to crap. "I had thought I was going to be a billionaire," Pierce says. "I had all this stock, and now it was worthless."

In the real world Pierce was just a 19-year-old washed-up child actor living far from home and going slowly broke. But in Norrath he was none of that. In Norrath he was the dark-elf wizard Athrex, and he was a champion. He played on *EverQuest*'s Vallon Zek server, by far the most competitive of the three dozen subcommunities into which the *EverQuest* player population was segregated, and even there he stood out. "There would be server-wide tournaments and I would win them," he says, proud even now of his skill in both combat and the endless grind of monster killing and gradual, relentless "leveling up" that defines MMOs.

Pierce was a pioneer of the art of "six-boxing": Hopping between half a dozen computers, he would run his dark elf and five little 3-D helpers through dungeons designed to kick the ass of all but the best-trained and best-equipped player groups. He got so good he could reliably kill the mushroom-headed Myconid Spore King, thus securing a regular supply of enchanted Fungi Tunics, which dropped from its corpse. In MMO-speak, Pierce was now single-handedly "farming" Fungi Tunics—acquiring them as a matter of routine. This coveted piece of armor sold for up to 50,000 Norrathian platinum pieces, an amount of virtual money that took most players a full 150 hours to earn. That much virtual loot could cost $500 on eBay.

Pierce knew how much real money his farming could have earned him. By then he was rising to prominence in Vallon Zek's premier guild, Twelve Prophets, led by Swiss 18-year-old Alan Debonneville, who in addition to managing the guild was selling *EverQuest* items and currency on the side. "I was in charge of the market on my server," Debonneville says. "I would net $6,000 to $8,000 per month."

Pierce had certainly thought about turning pro. Before DEN took off, in fact, he'd started a business in virtual trading cards in the online game *Sanctum* and had pulled down $30K a year. And it wasn't a legal issue: "There clearly was a market for selling virtual items for real money," Pierce says. "It was less clear that it was against the rules, and it was certainly not against the law anywhere." But what held Pierce back was a problem of scale: He still was looking for a way back to the multimillion-dollar business world he'd run away from, and somehow the $13-a-month fantasy world he'd run away to didn't seem like the place he'd find it. The kind of business it would take to fit Pierce's ambition—a truly corporate retailer of the virtual, complete with org chart, business plan, and potential IPO—was without precedent. It was a thing so improbable and awesome, come to think of it, that actually making it happen might redeem not just the years he'd lost to DEN but the additional year and a half he had now spent doing little else but play a videogame.

And once he finally did come to think of it that way, Pierce was playing a new game: making his redemption a reality. In May 2001, he founded IGE with what was left of his own savings, setting up corporate headquarters in a 700-square-foot office in downtown Marbella and hiring some locals to do the farming—to rack up *EverQuest* items he could sell for cash. The company's ultimate goal, Pierce says, was to shift to the far more efficient model of acquiring its supply entirely from freelance farmers—and within a few months, IGE would be doing just that. But first Pierce invited Debonneville down to Spain for a look around. There, as Debonneville would relate in a legal complaint several years later, Pierce introduced him to Collins-Rector and Shackley, explained that the three of them had made millions, and invited Debonneville to join him now in making millions more. "I told Alan this could be a $100 million business," Pierce says. "I had that vision."

Debonneville didn't hesitate. He moved to Spain and joined IGE with a 2 percent ownership stake and full responsibility for the management of sales, supply, and technology, thus freeing Pierce to concentrate on long-term strategy. And if, in the months that followed, Pierce was slow to give Debonneville a more detailed picture of his business background, well, who could blame him? [...]

[...] Yantis was old-school—as old-school as it was possible to be in a business as new as RMT. He was 31, and his Web site—MySuper Sales.com—had been the dominant *EverQuest* virtual retailer almost as long as *EverQuest* had been the dominant MMO. He was the competition to beat.

Yantis declined to participate in this article, but he spoke with me at length in 2002 about his business. He was netting roughly $2,500 a day—nearly $1 million in annual profit from an operation consisting of himself and an assistant working out of his house in Rosarito, Mexico. He also had maybe a dozen in-game delivery agents in places like Romania, working for the equivalent of $3.50 per delivery. They were the virtual-world equivalent of couriers, walking their avatars right up to the purchaser's avatar to hand over the in-game goods.

Yantis was the epitome of pre-IGE cottage-industry virtual retail: informal, personal, and very low-profile. He forbade his family to play *EverQuest*, and he never touched the game himself, on the theory that this made it harder for the gamemaker to trace his operations back to him. It also meant he never had to accept the license agreement that prohibited his business. Getting busted meant losing inventory, losing inventory meant losing money, and losing money wasn't what Yantis was about. He once went to Texas to confront a player who had cheated him on a trade. "I flew right in and took a taxi to his house, sat down with his parents, and got a check cut right there."

As long as Yantis got paid he really didn't care what people thought of him. Pierce, on the other hand, cared a lot, and by 2003, with his legal problems now cleared up, he started a campaign to win gaming-industry hearts and minds. I first met him and Debonneville that November at the State of Play conference on virtual worlds in New York City, where academic games researchers and MMO designers all stared slack-jawed at these smiling emissaries from what many still thought of as a semi-criminal underworld. The boys wore nice suits, handed out business cards, and clearly meant business. IGE had set up US headquarters in Boca Raton, Florida, but the real base of operations—mainly engaged in around-the-clock delivery of *EverQuest* items—was now in Hong Kong and soon would occupy two floors in the same building as AOL Time Warner Asia.

I was in the business myself at the time, selling items in the classic MMO *Ultima Online*. After the conference, I blogged "Brock Pierce looks like a Norman Rockwell 13-year-old, talks like a coked-up 35-year-old, and happens to have turned 23 last Friday. He is either my new best friend or my new worst nightmare." What alarmed me was the news that IGE was planning to move beyond *EverQuest* to other games—including *Ultima*. "I haven't even had a chance to get my little five-and-dime up and running," I lamented, "and already the Wal-Mart is coming to town."

But I was kidding myself if I thought I was even on IGE's radar. All its efforts were aimed at crushing Yantis. "It was a market-share game," Pierce says. If Yantis lowered his prices, IGE did, too. If Yantis sought to exploit his more-established reputation, IGE sought to bury him in Google AdWords. ("We were probably one of Google's largest advertisers," Pierce says, adding that they spent about $1 million a month on text ads touting their affordable *EverQuest* platinum.)

Yantis' great misstep, Pierce says, was not thinking big enough. "Jonathan believed that this would only be a market in *EverQuest*. We had successfully diversified; in *Final Fantasy XI*, we had a nice profit margin. We were able to bring our margins down in *EverQuest*. We said to him, 'We are going to bring this market to ruins unless you come join us.'"

IGE was still the underdog, but in the end it was Yantis who blinked. The press release went out on January 22, 2004: IGE and Yantis' MySuperSales site were merging. Yantis got payments totalling $2.4 million and a 37 percent stake in the new company, and he joined the team as chief operating officer. "After that, the money started to flow," Pierce says. "Very well."

For IGE, this was the beginning of an age of gold. Literally: *World of Warcraft* was released in November 2004, and over the next year the platinum of *EverQuest*'s Norrath was replaced by the gold of *WoW*'s Azeroth as the most heavily traded virtual currency in the world. *WoW*'s growth rate was phenomenal—the game now has 11 million subscribers, 20 times as much as *EverQuest* ever had—and the RMT markets grew with it. But most important, *WoW* did something that made IGE's decision to move to Hong Kong the year before look practically clairvoyant. It ushered in the era of the industrial Chinese gold farm.

According to industry lore, China's first gold farms sprang up as early as 2002 just across the border from Korea. MMOs were huge in that country, and it was supposedly Korean player-entrepreneurs who hit upon the idea of hiring low-wage Chinese workers to farm the currency and equipment that other users craved.

But in the end it was the huge new market of Western *WoW* players that gave thousands of small-time Chinese capitalists a reason to set up gold farms of their own. And when they did, it was IGE that became the Wal-Mart moving all that product west to gold-starved players. The Hong Kong base made IGE uniquely suited for the job, and soon the company had a new Shanghai supply center and a Web site just for Chinese suppliers; they could see what the offering price for gold was on a particular server. "We had over 100 people working in Shanghai," Debonneville says, and the investment was worth every cent, securing IGE a truly reliable supply chain—and the sweetened profits that went with it.

The source of those profits, ultimately, was operations like the one owned and operated by 26-year-old Liu Haibin in Jinhua, China, which I visited a few years ago. With about 30 workers on staff, Liu was able to keep a gold-farming setup running around the clock. While the night shift slept upstairs on plywood bunks, day-shift workers sat in the hot, dimly lit workshop, each tending three or four computers. They were "playing" *World of Warcraft*, farming gold at an impressive clip by hunting and looting monsters, their productivity greatly abetted by automated bots that allowed them to handle multiple characters with little effort. They worked 84-hour weeks, got a couple of days off per month, and earned about $4 a day, which even for China was not a stellar wage.

Liu's income was better but not always by much. "Sometimes in a month you can lose all the profit you made in a year," he said, admitting there were days he regretted getting into the business in the first place. Why bother? "We also love this game," Liu told me.

Most American *WoW* players at the time knew little about how the farmers lived and worked. What they did know was that there seemed to be more and more of them in the game (broken English and repetitive playing patterns gave them away) and that *WoW*'s publisher, Blizzard Entertainment, did not look favorably on their presence. A Blizzard policy statement reads: "They spam advertisements, use bots that make it hard for players to find the resources they need, and raise the cost of items through inflation." As the gold-farmer population grew, opponents flooded message boards with anti-Chinese invective and increasingly took note of the role a company called IGE seemed to play in the phenomenon.

The company was drawing more attention elsewhere, too. When Pierce and Debonneville returned to New York for the second State of Play conference, they came with an entourage. There was Yantis, now part of the team and looking not especially comfortable in the position. And there was a fiftysomething named Steve Salyer, a former Electronic Arts executive who had just been hired as IGE's president—and who made the eye-popping announcement there that the RMT business was now an $880 million industry.

"There's no question in my mind that in the future millions of people will make their living in cyberspace," Salyer told me soon thereafter, doing his best to sell the significance of the virtual gold trade in general—and IGE in particular. His job, after all, was to get the company taken seriously. The IGE founders had built a successful business, and now they wanted to make it a legitimate one: IGE wanted deals with game publishers that would give it license to traffic in virtual items without violating the games' terms of service. That sort of deal wasn't likely to get cut with a couple of college-age unknowns. As Debonneville put it, "Brock and I were not adult faces." [...]

[...] In the months ahead, IGE hired more adults, a slew of VPs with decades of industry experience among them. The company also brought on a former Goldman Sachs investment banker named Stephen Bannon, whose mission was to land venture capital.

By spring 2005, Yantis was telling IGE affiliates that the company would be announcing limited licensing agreements permitting it to operate aboveboard in at least five North American MMOs. Yantis himself, however, wouldn't be sticking around to see it happen. Pierce and Yantis had arrived at, as Pierce puts it, a "difference of opinion," and in June, after months of negotiation, the terms of Yantis' exit were finalized: For 22 monthly payments of $1 million each, the company would get Yantis' stake back, along with his agreement not to set up a competing business for at least three years.

Goldman Sachs started making visits, inspecting the Asian operations and talking with Bannon and others about terms. Finally, on February 7, 2006, the deal was inked: Goldman Sachs, together with a consortium of private funds, made a reported $60 million investment in the company. Part of the money was used to buy Pierce, Salyer, and IGE's general counsel, Randy Maslow, out of some of their stock in the company. Pierce walked away with $20 million and still retained the controlling share of a company that was doing more than a quarter of a billion dollars in sales a year. The only top IGE officer who failed to profit from the deal was Debonneville, who, for reasons that remain disputed, was excluded from selling any part of the 17 percent stake he'd built up. Two and a half months later, he left the company.

For Pierce, this was a moment to savor. But it was a short one. Even before the Goldman Sachs deal was sealed, profits had started declining, and by December 2005 IGE defaulted on its monthly payment to Yantis. The company was obliged to waive the noncompete agreement and let Yantis set up his own virtual currency site, which he made clear would be dedicated to crushing IGE.

Nor was Yantis the only new opposition IGE was facing. By mid 2006, Blizzard Entertainment was cracking down harder than ever on gold farmers and sellers, shutting accounts by the thousands. The moves cost IGE as much as $200,000 in inventory every month, to say nothing of the havoc it played with suppliers. By January 2007, the company's RMT operation was losing more than half a million dollars a month.

At one time, Pierce might have shrugged off those losses, confident that any day the MMO industry would cave in to its customers' unquenchable desire for loot and authorize IGE to provide it. But it had now been over a year since those big licensing deals were supposed to have been announced. And where were they? Nowadays, the few game companies that even admit to having had conversations with IGE deny they ever came close to a deal. "IGE approached us on several occasions," says John Smedley, president of *EverQuest*'s parent, Sony Online Entertainment, "but we flat out turned them down." As for Blizzard, one approach was plenty. David Christensen, then IGE's VP of business development, wrangled a meeting with them, but the company wouldn't even let him on the premises for it. "They took him to a ball game or something, and he got like 10 minutes with them," a former IGE manager recalls. "'They basically hate us' was what he related afterward."

Things weren't all bad. The investment money allowed IGE to make some sound diversifying moves, acquiring the very profitable South Korean real-money exchange site Itemmania, a sort of player-to-player eBay for virtual items. But for IGE's retail trading operations—long the core of the company and its main source of income—things didn't look like they could possibly get worse.

And then they did.

On May 30, 2007, a 28-year-old gamer named Antonio Hernandez filed a multimillion-dollar class-action lawsuit against IGE in a U.S. district court in Florida. Hernandez was a *World of Warcraft* diehard, averaging by his own description 35 to 40 hours a week of play, and it was on behalf of almost every other *WoW* player in the U.S. that he was suing IGE for "substantially impairing" and "diminishing" their collective enjoyment of the game. Specifically, Hernandez held IGE responsible for every ill that could be attributed to RMT in general and gold farming in particular, and he was using the leverage of consumer-protection law to make the company answer for it. As Hernandez's attorney, Richard Newsome, explained the case to a reporter: "Guys like Tony have paid their $15 for some entertainment, and IGE is polluting that entertainment. It's kind of like if someone pays for a ticket to go see a movie and someone else comes in behind them and kicks their seat."

Hernandez wanted IGE to stop selling virtual merchandise, but that was just the start of it. In addition to a court order enjoining IGE from selling *World of Warcraft* goods, he was asking the judge for monetary damages—compensation for millions of *WoW* account holders in the U.S., plus double that to make it hurt, and just in case that wasn't pain enough, a further payout of every penny the company had ever earned through its "wrongful conduct," which pretty much meant every penny it had ever earned. In effect, Hernandez was seeking not just to punish IGE but to extinguish it.

He might have even succeeded, except for one thing: You can't kill something that's already dead. Though neither Hernandez nor his lawyers could have known it, the Florida-based company he was suing, IGE US, was no longer what it used to be. Just two months before the suit was filed, Pierce had acceded to the inevitable and cut loose the company's hemorrhaging retail operation, selling it at a deep discount (for a mid-seven-figure royalty agreement) to the only potential buyer capable of doing anything productive with it: Jonathan Yantis.

The business on which IGE was built was sold off, and the company shed its name, becoming Affinity Media and redefining itself as a marketer of the MMO community sites it once bought just to boost its own traffic. IGE US persisted, but only as a holding company with no holdings other than a minority stake in Affinity. It was empty now, a husk.

IGE.com persisted as well and remained, as it remains today, among the top virtual-currency sites. But it belonged to Yantis now, who owned it through a web of companies registered in places like Vanuatu and Australia and more resistant to lawsuits like Hernandez's. It took Yantis a while to sort out the mess Pierce had left behind. Many suppliers had gone unpaid and were still harassing the former IGE Shanghai for payment. In May, according to a rumor that made the rounds of MMO blogs, a desperate gold-farm operator stormed the IGE Shanghai offices demanding 2 million yuan and using a "toy pistol" to hold employees hostage.

But accounts were settled in the end, and new practices stabilized the supply chain. "Basically," says James Clarke, a veteran turnaround executive who replaced Debonneville as IGE's COO (and left the company last January), "what happens now is that the risk has been pushed further up the supply chain. Retailers often don't even touch the gold; they don't even have accounts anymore. It's the farmer that holds the gold and risks the banning."

This was not a great way for Pierce to start the year—and the year never got much better. In June, he was forced out as CEO of Affinity and replaced by Stephen Bannon, the investment banker who had joined the board when the Goldman Sachs deal went through. That same month, Debonneville sued Pierce in Los Angeles federal court, seeking millions of dollars in damages for "breaches of fiduciary duty, breaches of contract, and fraud" related to Debonneville's exclusion from the Goldman buyout—and dredging up questions of character that reached all the way back to the DEN days. A few months later, as if on cue, Collins-Rector made British tabloid news when he reportedly turned up in London consorting with teenage boys ("Tycoon Paedo on Prowl in UK" blared one headline). Debonneville's court filings, meanwhile, revealed that the year before, Pierce had told him that Collins-Rector was blackmailing him, threatening to snarl IGE in litigation that would make it unattractive to investors. Debonneville's suit was settled before it got to court. By the year's end, it looked like Pierce might never really escape the shadows of his past.

But by then it was clear that Pierce's undoing had also been the result of uncertainties about the nature of virtual goods in general. Who really owns them? Who determines their value? These are the kinds of questions that a case like Hernandez's should have helped resolve. And as long as they remain unsettled, no game company will ever let any single independent entity control the amounts of virtual wealth that Pierce and IGE once did.

Not that Steve Salyer was wrong to suggest that one day "millions" would be earning a living in the markets IGE pioneered (already the number doing so in China has reached the hundreds of thousands). Or that Pierce was wrong to think that MMO publishers would one day accept the inevitability of RMT in some form or another. In the past year, there's been accelerated movement toward publisher-sanctioned item sales: Funcom, makers of the new MMO *Age of Conan*, and Sony Online Entertainment have both announced partnerships with a startup called Live Gamer to provide player-to-player RMT exchange sites. At the same time, the so-called free-to-play model—no subscription fees, revenue derived entirely from direct sales of in-game items—has made inroads in the Asian MMO market and is being embraced by no less a gaming giant than Electronic Arts in the upcoming *Battlefield Heroes*. But both these models, in their blunt rejection of IGE's third-party retail model, only underline what Pierce himself implicitly conceded when he sold out to Yantis: There is no future for his once-bright dream except in the dimness of what is plainly now a permanent gray market.

As for Pierce, whatever regrets he may have about the way things ended lie hidden behind that familiar smile and a steady stream of upbeat Facebook status updates ("Brock is having a super day!"). He's back in the startup game, he says, working on a social network aimed at wine lovers like himself. But his IGE chapter is closed. Antonio Hernandez made sure of that much, however little else he achieved. When he and his legal team finally figured out the nature of what they were suing, they realized there was nothing to do but settle for the best terms they could get, and in August, finally, the deal was announced. In return for dismissal, the defendant agreed to Hernandez's central demand: IGE US, already just a corporate ghost—a static afterimage of the vision Pierce had long ago wrested from the depths of his obsession with the game—was now legally barred from having anything to do with the sale of Azerothian gold for real money until the year 2013.

Investigate the world of online gaming commerce. Can you find (or do you know of) sites that sell, for real money, items "made entirely of fiction and code" (page 141). What other monetary expenditures might we incur in our lives for items equally intangible or fictional? What other expenditures—of time, energy, or emotion—do people make in online gaming and virtual reality settings?

Make a hypothetical argument that buying a *World of Warcraft* weapon is *just as real* as buying an actual gun. Then, with logic and evidence to support your premises, make an argument that it's a *fundamentally different* transaction. Try again, contrasting your virtual weaponry purchase with a song on iTunes, a video download, or a work of art. What gives these items value?

Dibbell describes a world of competitive (or questionable) business practices; entrepreneurial "gold farms" (or sweatshops); an obsessive, scandal-plagued teenager (or internet mogul); and lawsuits alleging "wrongful conduct" (or the diminishment of enjoyment). Which of these issues seem real? With your group, generate a list of the supposed ethical problems that arise throughout this article and analyze them. What value system are you imposing as you decide which behaviors transgress ethical conduct and which do not.

CALVIN & HOBBES
WALKING BILLBOARD

By Bill Watterson

Panel 1: I WISH MY SHIRT HAD A LOGO OR A PRODUCT ON IT.

Panel 2: A GOOD SHIRT TURNS THE WEARER INTO A WALKING CORPORATE BILLBOARD!

Panel 3: IT SAYS TO THE WORLD, "MY IDENTITY IS SO WRAPPED UP IN WHAT I BUY THAT *I* PAID THE *COMPANY* TO ADVERTISE ITS PRODUCTS!"

Panel 4: YOU'D ADMIT THAT? / OH SURE. ENDORSING PRODUCTS IS THE AMERICAN WAY TO EXPRESS INDIVIDUALITY.

© 1992 Watterson/Distributed by Universal Press Syndicate

This comic strip's argument is made through irony. What is the argument Watterson is making and how is he using irony?

In your group, list the companies you are advertising for (that is, what corporate, business, or commercial logos and images are you and your group mates sporting). Assign $100 for large logos, $50 for medium, and $25 for small. Multiply the price by the number of logos. Compare all the groups in the class to find the one that is giving away the most in free advertising.

excerpt from

CATCH-22

BY JOSEPH HELLER

MILO

April had been the best month of all for Milo. Lilacs bloomed in April and fruit ripened on the vine. Heartbeats quickened and old appetites were renewed. In April a livelier iris gleamed upon the burnished dove. April was spring, and in the spring Milo Minderbinder's[1] fancy had lightly turned to thoughts of tangerines.

"Tangerines?"

"Yes, sir."

"My men would love tangerines," admitted the colonel in Sardinia who commanded four squadrons of B-26s.

"There'll be all the tangerines they can eat that you're able to pay for with money from your mess fund," Milo assured him.

"Casaba melons?"

"Are going for a song in Damascus."

"I have a weakness for casaba melons. I've always had a weakness for casaba melons."

"Just lend me one plane from each squadron, just one plane, and you'll have all the casabas you can eat that you've money to pay for."

"We buy from the syndicate?"

"And everybody has a share."

"It's amazing, positively amazing. How can you do it?"

"Mass purchasing power makes the big difference. For example, breaded veal cutlets."

"I'm not so crazy about breaded veal cutlets," grumbled the skeptical B-25 commander in the north of Corsica.

"Breaded veal cutlets are very nutritious," Milo admonished him piously. "They contain egg yolk and bread crumbs. And so are lamb chops."

"Ah, lamb chops," echoed the B-25 commander. "Good lamb chops?"

"The best," said Milo, "that the black market has to offer."

"Baby lamb chops?"

"In the cutest little pink paper panties you ever saw. Are going for a song in Portugal."

"I can't send a plane to Portugal. I haven't the authority."

"I can, once you lend the plane to me. With a pilot to fly it. And don't forget—you'll get General Dreedle."[2]

"Will General Dreedle eat in my mess hall again?"

"Like a pig, once you start feeding him my best white fresh eggs fried in my pure creamery butter. There'll be tangerines too, and casaba melons, honeydews, filet of Dover sole, baked Alaska, and cockles and mussels."

"And everybody has a share?"

"That," said Milo, "is the most beautiful part of it."

"I don't like it," growled the uncooperative fighter-plane commander, who didn't like Milo either.

"There's an uncooperative fighter-plane commander up north who's got it in for me," Milo complained to General Dreedle. "It takes just one person to ruin the whole thing, and then you wouldn't have your fresh eggs fried in my pure creamery butter anymore."

General Dreedle had the uncooperative fighter-plane commander transferred to the Solomon Islands to dig graves and replaced him with a senile colonel with bursitis and a craving for litchi nuts who introduced Milo to the B-17 general on the mainland with a yearning for Polish sausage.

"Polish sausage is going for peanuts in Cracow," Milo informed him.

"Polish sausage," sighed the general nostalgically. "You know, I'd give just about anything for a good hunk of Polish sausage. Just about anything."

"You don't have to give *anything*. Just give me one plane for each mess hall and a pilot who will do what he's told. And a small down payment on your initial order as a token of good faith."

"But Cracow is hundreds of miles behind enemy lines. How will you get the sausage?"

"There's an international Polish sausage exchange in Geneva. I'll just fly the peanuts into Switzerland and exchange them for Polish sausage at the open market rate. They'll fly the peanuts back to Cracow and I'll fly the Polish sausage back to you. You buy only as much Polish sausage as you want through the syndicate. There'll be tangerines too, with only a little artificial coloring added. And eggs from Malta and Scotch from Sicily. You'll be paying the money to yourself when you buy from the syndicate, since you'll own a share, so you'll really be getting everything you buy for nothing. Doesn't that make sense?"

"Sheer genius. How in the world did you ever think of it?"

"My name is Milo Minderbinder. I am twenty-seven years old."

Milo Minderbinder's planes flew in from everywhere, the pursuit planes, bombers, and cargo ships streaming into Colonel Cathcart's[3] field with pilots at the controls who would do what they were told. The planes were decorated with flamboyant squadron emblems illustrating such laudable ideals as Courage, Might, Justice, Truth, Liberty, Love, Honor and Patriotism that were painted out at once by Milo's mechanics with a double coat of flat white and replaced in garish purple with the stenciled name M & M Enterprises, Fine Fruits and Produce. The "M & M" in "M & M Enterprises" stood for Milo & Minderbinder, and the & was inserted, Milo revealed candidly, to nullify any impression that the syndicate was a one-man operation. Planes arrived for Milo from airfields in Italy, North Africa and England, and from Air Transport Command stations in Liberia, Ascension Island, Cairo and Karachi. Pursuit planes were traded for additional cargo ships or retained for emergency invoice duty and small-parcel service; trucks and tanks were procured from the ground forces and used to short-distance road hauling. Everybody had a share, and men got fat and moved about tamely with toothpicks in their greasy lips. Milo supervised the whole expanding operation by himself. Deep otter-brown lines of preoccupation etched themselves permanently into his careworn face and gave him a harried look of sobriety and mistrust. Everybody but Yossarian thought Milo was a jerk, first for volunteering for the job of mess officer and next for taking it so seriously. Yossarian[4] also thought that Milo was a jerk; but he also knew that Milo was a genius.

One day Milo flew away to England to pick up a load of Turkish halvah and came flying back from Madagascar leading four German bombers filled with yams, collards, mustard greens and black-eyed Georgia peas. Milo was dumbfounded when he stepped down to the ground and found a contingent of armed M.P.s waiting to imprison the German pilots and confiscate their planes. *Confiscate!* The mere word was anathema to him, and he stormed back and forth in excoriating condemnation, shaking a piercing finger of rebuke in the guilt-ridden faces of Colonel Cathcart, Colonel Korn[5] and the poor battle-scarred captain with the submachine gun who commanded the M.P.s.

"Is this Russia?" Milo assailed them incredulously at the top of his voice. "*Confiscate?*" he shrieked, as though he could not believe his own ears. "Since when is it the policy of the American government to confiscate the private property of its citizens? Shame on all of you for even thinking such a horrible thought."

"But Milo," Major Danby[6] interrupted timidly, "We're at war with Germany, and those are German planes."

"They are no such thing!" Milo retorted furiously. "Those planes belong to the syndicate, and everybody has a share. *Confiscate?* How can you possibly confiscate your own private property? *Confiscate*, indeed! I've never heard of anything so depraved in my whole life."

And sure enough, Milo was right, for when they looked, his mechanics had painted out the German swastikas on the wings, tails and fuselages with double coats of flat white and stenciled in the words **M & M Enterprises, Fine Fruits and Produce**. Right before their eyes he had transformed his syndicate into an international cartel.

Milo's argosies[7] of plenty now filled the air. Planes poured in from Norway, Denmark, France, Germany, Austria, Italy, Yugoslavia, Romania, Bulgaria, Sweden, Finland, Poland—from everywhere in Europe, in fact, but Russia, with whom Milo refused to do business. When everybody who was going to had signed up with **M & M Enterprises, Fine Fruits and Produce**, Milo created a wholly owned subsidiary, **M & M Enterprises, Fancy Pastry**, and obtained more airplanes and more money from the mess funds for scones and crumpets from the British Isles, prune and cheese Danish from Copenhagen, éclairs, cream puffs, Napoleons and *petits fours* from Paris, Reims and Grenoble, *Kugelbopf*, pumpernickel and *Pfefferkuchen* from Berlin, *Linzer* and *Dobos Torten* from Vienna, *Strudel* from Hungary and *Baklava* from Ankara. Each morning Milo sent planes aloft all over Europe and North Africa hauling long red tow signs advertising the day's specials in large square letters: "eye round, 79¢... whiting, 21¢." He boosted cash income for the syndicate by leasing tow signs to Pet Milk, Gaines Dog Food, and Noxzema. In a spirit of civic enterprise, he regularly allotted a certain amount of free aerial advertising space to General Peckem[8] for the propagation of such messages in the public interest as NEATNESS COUNTS, HASTE MAKES WASTE, and the FAMILY THAT PRAYS TOGETHER STAYS TOGETHER. Milo purchased spot radio announcements on Axis Sally's and Lord Haw Haw's daily propaganda broadcasts from Berlin to keep things moving. Business boomed on every battlefront.

Milo's planes were a familiar sight. They had freedom of passage everywhere, and one day Milo contracted with the American military authorities to bomb the German-held highway bridge at Orvieto and with the German military authorities to defend the highway bridge at Orvieto with anti-aircraft fire against his own attack. His fee for attacking the bridge for America was the total cost of the operation plus six percent, and his fee from Germany for defending the bridge was the same cost-plus-six agreement augmented by a merit bonus of a thousand dollars for every American plane he shot down. The consummation of these deals represented an important victory for private enterprise, he pointed out, since the armies of both countries were socialized institutions. Once the contracts were signed there seemed to be no point in using the resources of the syndicate to bomb and defend the bridge, inasmuch as both governments had ample men and material right there to do so and were perfectly happy to contribute them, and in the end Milo realized a fantastic profit from both halves of his project for doing nothing more than signing his name twice.

The arrangements were fair to both sides. Since Milo did have freedom of passage everywhere, his planes were able to steal over in a sneak attack without alerting the German anti-aircraft gunners, and since Milo knew about the attack, he was able to alert the German anti-aircraft gunners in sufficient time for them to begin firing accurately the moment the planes came into range. It was an ideal arrangement for everyone but the dead man in Yossarian's tent, who was killed over the garget the day he arrived.

"I didn't kill him!" Milo kept replying passionately to Yossarian's angry protest. "I wasn't even there that day, I tell you. Do you think I was down there on the ground firing an anti-aircraft gun when the planes came over?"

"But you organized the whole thing, didn't you?" Yossarian shouted back at him in the velvet darkness cloaking the path leading past the still vehicles of the motor pool to the open-air movie theater.

"And I didn't organize anything," Milo answered indignantly, drawing great agitated sniffs of air in through his hissing, pale, twitching nose. "The Germans have the bridge, and we were going to bomb it, whether I stepped into the picture or not. I just saw a wonderful opportunity to make some profit out of the mission, and I took it. What's so terrible about that?"

"What's so terrible about it? Milo, a man in my tent was killed on that mission before he could even unpack his bags."

"But I didn't kill him."

"You got a thousand dollars extra for it."

"But I didn't kill him. I wasn't even there, I tell you. I was in Barcelona buying olive oil and skinless and boneless sardines, and I've got the purchase orders to prove it. And I didn't get the thousand dollars. That thousand dollars went to the syndicate, and everybody got a share, even you." Milo was appealing to Yossarian from the bottom of his soul. "Look, I didn't start this war, Yossarian, no matter what that lousy Wintergreen[9] is saying. I'm just trying to put it on a businesslike basis. Is anything wrong with that? You know, a thousand dollars ain't such a bad price for a medium bomber and a crew. If I can persuade the Germans to pay me a thousand dollars for every plane they shoot down, why shouldn't I take it?"

"Because you're dealing with the enemy, that's why. Can't you understand that we're fighting a war? People are dying. Look around you, for Christ's sake!"

Milo shook his head with weary forbearance. "And the Germans are not our enemies," he declared. "Oh, and I know what you're going to say. Sure, we're at war with them. But the Germans are also members in good standing of the syndicate, and it's my job to protect their rights as shareholders. Maybe they did start the war, and maybe they are killing millions of people, but they pay their bills a lot more promptly than some allies of ours I could name. Don't you understand that I have to respect the sanctity of my contract with Germany? Can't you see it from my point of view?"

"No," Yossarian rebuffed him harshly.

Milo was stung and made no effort to disguise his wounded feelings. It was a muggy, moonlit night filled with gnats, moths, and mosquitoes. Milo lifted his arm suddenly and pointed toward the open-air theater, where the milky, dust-filled beam bursting horizontally from the projector slashed a conelike swath in the blackness and draped in a fluorescent membrane of light the audience tilted on the seats there in hypnotic sags, their faces focused upward toward the aluminized movie screen. Milo's eyes were liquid with integrity, and his artless and uncorrupted face was lustrous with a shining mixture of sweat and insect repellent.

"Look at them," he exclaimed in a voice choked with emotion. "They're my friends, my countrymen, my comrades in arms. A fellow never had a better bunch of buddies. Do you think I'd do a single thing to harm them if I didn't have to? Haven't I got enough on my mind? Can't you see how upset I am already about all that cotton piling up on those piers in Egypt?" Milo's voice splintered into fragments, and he clutched at Yossarian's shirt front as though drowning. His eyes were throbbing visibly like brown caterpillars. "Yossarian, what am I going to do with so much cotton? It's all your fault for letting me buy it." […]

[…] M & M Enterprises verged on collapse. Milo cursed himself hourly for his monumental greed and stupidity in purchasing the entire Egyptian cotton crop, but a contract was a contract and had to be honored, and one night, after a sumptuous evening meal, all Milo's fighters and bombers took off, joined in formation directly overhead and began dropping bombs on the group. He had landed another contract with the Germans this time to bomb his own outfit. Milo's planes separated in a well-coordinated attack and bombed the fuel stocks and the ordnance dump, the repair hangars and the B-25 bombers resting on the lollipop shaped hardstands at the field. His crews spared the landing strip and the mess halls so that they could land safely when their work was done and enjoy a hot snack before retiring. They bombed with their landing lights on, since no one was shooting back. They bombed all four squadrons, the officer's club and the Group Headquarters building. Men bolted from their tents in sheer terror and did not know in which direction to turn. Wounded soon lay screaming everywhere. A cluster of fragmentation bombs exploded in the yard of the officers' club and punched jagged holes in the side of the wooden building and in the bellies and backs of a row of lieutenants and captains standing at the bar. They doubled over in agony and dropped. The rest of the officers fled toward the two exits in panic and jammed up the doorways like a dense, howling dam of human flesh as they shrank from going farther.

Colonel Cathcart clawed and elbowed his way through the unruly, bewildered mass until he stood outside by himself. He stared up at the sky in stark astonishment and horror. Milo's planes, ballooning serenely in over the blossoming treetops with their bomb bay doors open and wing flaps down and with their monstrous, bug-eyed, blinding, fiercely flickering, eerie landing lights on, were the most apocalyptic sight he had ever beheld. Colonel Cathcart let go a stricken gasp of dismay and hurled himself headlong into his jeep, almost sobbing. He found the gas pedal and the ignition and sped toward the airfield as fast as the rocking car would carry him, his huge flabby hands clenched and bloodless on the wheel or blaring his horn tormentedly. Once he almost killed himself when he swerved with a banshee screech of tires to avoid plowing into a bunch of men running crazily toward the hills in their underwear with their stunned faces down and their thin arms pressed high around their temples as puny shields. Yellow, orange and red fires were burning on both sides of the road. Tents and trees were in flames, and Milo's planes kept coming around interminably with their blinking white landing lights on and their bomb bay doors open. Colonel Cathcart almost turned his jeep over when he slammed the brakes on at the control tower. He leaped from the car while it was still skidding dangerously and hurtled up the flight of steps inside, where three men were busy at the instruments and the controls. He bowled two of them aside in his lunge for the nickel-plated microphone, his eyes glittering wildly and his beefy face contorted with stress. He squeezed the microphone in a bestial grip and began shouting hysterically at the top of his voice, "Milo, you son of a bitch! Are you crazy? What the hell are you doing? Come down! Come down!"

"Stop hollering so much, will you?" answered Milo, who was standing there right beside him in the control tower with a microphone of his own. "I'm right here." Milo looked at him with reproof and turned back to his work. "Very good, men, very good," he chanted into his microphone. "But I see one supply shed still standing. That will never do, Purvis—I've spoken to you about that kind of shoddy work before. Now, you go right back there this minute and try it again. And this time come in slowly...slowly. Haste makes waste, Purvis. Haste makes waste. If I've told you once, I must have told you a hundred times. Haste makes waste."

The loud-speaker overhead began squawking. "Milo, this is Alvin Brown. I've finished dropping my bombs. What should I do now?"

"Strafe," said Milo.

"Strafe?" Alvin Brown was shocked.

"We have no choice," Milo informed him resignedly. "It's in the contract."

"Oh, okay, then," Alvin Brown acquiesced. "In that case I'll strafe."

This time Milo had gone too far. Bombing his own men and planes was more than even the most phlegmatic observer could stomach, and it looked like the end for him. High-ranking government officials poured in to investigate. Newspapers inveighed against Milo with glaring headlines, and Congressmen denounced the atrocity in stentorian wrath and clamored for punishment. Mothers with children in the service organized into militant groups and demanded revenge. Not one voice was raised in his defense. Decent people everywhere were affronted, and Milo was all washed up until he opened his books to the public and disclosed the tremendous profit he had made. He could reimburse the government for all the people and property he had destroyed and still have enough money left over to continue buying Egyptian cotton. Everybody, of course, owned a share. And the sweetest part of the whole deal was that there really was no need to reimburse the government at all.

"In a democracy, the government is the people," Milo explained. "We're people, aren't we? So we might just as well keep the money and eliminate the middleman. Frankly, I'd like to see the government get out of war altogether and leave the whole field to private industry. If we pay the government everything we owe it, we'll only be encouraging government control and discouraging other individuals from bombing their own men and planes. We'll be taking away their incentive." […]

ANNOTATIONS

1. Milo Minderbinder is the mess officer for the squadron: the officer in charge of feeding the troops

2. General Dreedle is the base commander

3. Colonel Cathcart is the group commander, under General Dreedle. He is genuinely disliked by most of the squadron because he keeps raising the number of missions men have to fly before they can rotate back to the U.S.

4. John Yossarian is the protagonist of the novel. He is a bombardier on a B-25. He finds the war absurd.

5. Colonel Korn is Colonel Carthcart's assistant.

6. Major Danby briefs flight crews on the missions they are to fly.

7. A rich supply fleet.

8. General Peckem is General Dreedle's rival.

9. Ex-PFC Wintergreen is in charge of the mail and, ironically, has power far above his station.

This passage famously satirizes the notion of an economics that supersedes ethics. In your opinion, what ethical principles (if any) ought to govern business? Do the same principles govern your day-to-day commerce? In what specific ways do you think this question is current; in other words, what specific issues do we face today that seem to demand an ethics of buying and selling?

Milo Minderbinder quells controversy at the end of this excerpt by agreeing to "reimburse" the government for the men he's killed. This is satire, sure, but does our society ever really put a price on human life? Regularly, the Internet features articles claiming to have totaled the cost of raising a child; insurance companies daily calculate the costs of elder care, disability injuries, and the like. In what other ways do we put price tags on human life? Is it always sinister? Find some examples and compare their supposed value systems or priorities.

Besides satirizing soulless capitalism, this excerpt seems to ridicule global capitalism, particularly when it clashes with nationalism in wartime. Milo, in other words, is not just a businessman without ethics, he's a traitor to his country. Write a paragraph in which you consider national identity in economic terms—"buy American" campaigns, for instance, or advertisements for American cars. Do you think of your identity—including your attitudes, behaviors, and desires toward material goods—more shaped by patriotism or economic ideology?

Thomas Greco is a community economist and monetary theorist. His 2009 book The End of Money and the Future of Civilization *investigates the history of money to point out what he sees as problems in the current economic system. He advocates alternate systems of exchange as a way to bring more stability and fairness to an economic system he sees as inequitable, opaque, and corrupt.*

excerpt from

THE EVOLUTION OF MONEY—FROM COMMODITY MONEY TO CREDIT MONEY

By Thomas H. Greco

It was in a dusty old bookshop close to the British Museum in London that I discovered a slim volume that was to complete for me the picture of how money has evolved over time. I had been traveling in Europe and the United Kingdom in the summer of 2001 with my then partner, Donna, partly to attend conferences in Germany and England, partly to spend time with friends and cohorts, and partly to do a bit of touring. It was actually Donna who discovered the book in the basement stacks and brought it to me, saying "what about this one?" The book was *The Meaning of Money* by Hartley Withers. Although I had already been engaged in intensive research into the subjects of money and banking for more than twenty years, and had written three books of my own on the subject, I had not previously heard of Withers. It was evident that Withers must have been, in his day, a recognized authority on the subject and that his book must have served for a long time as a leading text. I surmised that from the fact that the volume I held in my hands was the seventh edition, published in 1947, of a work that was first published in 1909. Reading Withers crystallized my understanding of the double transformation that money had undergone during the previous three hundred years, and understanding that allowed a clearer comprehension of the nature and significance of the changes that have taken place and that prepares the ground from which to launch the next great improvement in the exchange process.

WHAT WE DON'T KNOW IS HURTING US

Money is clouded in mystery and there are few who really understand it. It is not that it is so difficult to understand, but because it is made to seem that way by financial journalists, bankers, and monetary economists who speak an obscure language, indulge in superficial speculations about markets and policy changes, and behave as if the wizards of Wall Street were possessed of some superior form of intelligence. This discourages most people from even trying to understand money. But what we don't know can hurt us, and it is this general ignorance that is at the root of much of the present misery in the world. As John Adams, the second president of the United States, expressed it in a letter to Thomas Jefferson, "All the perplexities, confusions and distresses in America arise not from defects in the Constitution or Confederation, not from want of honor or virtue, as much as from downright ignorance of the nature of coin, credit and circulation." That is probably even more true in our present day than it was in the late eighteenth century.

Money is a human contrivance created to serve particular purposes, primarily to facilitate the exchange of goods and services. In this chapter, we will dispel the mystery by telling the story of money in a way that clearly distinguishes the various kinds of money and reveals their essential nature. We will explain the transformational stages through which money (or more accurately, the exchange process) has passed, and in the following chapter how it is once again being transformed. Subsequent chapters will describe the more efficient and equitable exchange mechanisms that are now emerging, and will suggest how they might be further perfected. For this, we need not speculate about the distant past, nor seek to uncover the obscure origins of money in ancient societies. It will suffice to examine how money and banking have evolved together over the past three hundred years.

KINDS OF ECONOMIC INTERACTION

To begin with, it is necessary to realize the precise role that money is intended to play. To do that, we must distinguish among the various modes by which real economic value changes hands. These are as follows:

- Gifts
- Involuntary transfers

- Reciprocal exchange

In the case of a gift, if it is truly a gift, something of value is transferred without any particular expectation of the giver receiving anything in return. In the case of involuntary transfers (such as theft, robbery, extortion, or taxes) some form of force or threat is applied to coerce the transfer of value from one person or entity to another. In reciprocal exchange, two parties voluntarily agree to exchange one value for another. Each, ostensibly, values the thing received more than the thing surrendered, so both are enriched by the bargain.

It is within the realm of reciprocal exchange that money plays its fundamental role as a *medium of exchange* or means of payment. Any feature of a monetary system that subverts reciprocity is dishonest and destructive to the intended outcome of mutual benefit among those who use money.

THE LADDER OF ECONOMIC CIVILIZATION

The key to understanding money lies in being able to distinguish between its mere *forms* on the one hand, and its true *essence* on the other. We often hear that money evolved from gold and silver coin, to paper money, to "checkbook money." But that does not really tell the story. Such a progression confuses money's forms with its essences. What we really need to know is the value basis of money in each of its historical manifestations. Paper is not the essence of paper money, but only the carrier of information. The nature of that information is what we shall describe shortly.

The process of reciprocal exchange has, over the centuries, evolved through numerous stages of what Withers has called "the ladder of economic civilization." It is extremely instructive to trace this evolution and to realize how money has repeatedly been transformed. Here, in sum, are the steps, each of which will be discussed in turn.

- Barter trade
- Commodity money
- Symbolic money
- Credit money
- Credit clearing

THE FIRST EVOLUTIONARY STEP—BARTER TO COMMODITY MONEY

The first step in the process of reciprocal exchange was from simple barter to commodity money. Barter is the most primitive form of reciprocal exchange. Barter involves only two people, each of which has something the other wants. However, if Jones wants something from Smith, but has nothing that Smith wants, there can be no barter trade. So barter depends upon the "double coincidence" of wants and needs. Money, in its most fundamental role, enables traders to transcend this barter limitation. Money bridges the gap in both space and time, acting as a "placeholder" that enables the need of a buyer to be met wherever and whenever the needed good or service may be found. This requires the agreement of the seller to defer satisfaction and to find his needed goods or services elsewhere. Thus, the first evolutionary step in reciprocal exchange came when traders began to use as an exchange medium some useful commodity that was in general demand and could be easily passed along in payment to other sellers.

COMMODITY MONEY

The most primitive type of money, then, is commodity money. Commodity money carries value in itself and can fulfill all the classical functions attributed to money. It is at once a payment medium, a measure of value, and a store of value. Throughout history, a wide variety of commodities has served as money including cattle, tobacco, grains, nails, shells, hides, and (of course) metals—especially the so-called precious metals, gold and silver. I may personally have no use for tobacco, but if there are many others who want it, I will accept it in payment for the things I sell because I know that I can use it later to pay for something I want. So some commodities acquired "exchange value" as well as "use value." But by using commodities as money, the transaction essentially remained a barter trade of one thing for another.

Because they are durable, portable, and easy to divide into smaller amounts (fungible), certain metals (notably silver and gold) became commodities of choice for mediating the exchange of all other goods and services. Eventually, these metals were struck (minted) into pieces (coins) of certified weight and purity (fineness) as a way of obviating the need for sellers to weigh and assay in the market the metal that was offered as payment. The certification may have been made by some trusted person or entity. There are many examples of private coinage, but more often coinage was claimed as a prerogative of the local political authority, a prince or a king, because there were good profits to be made from it. Official certification, if it could be relied upon increased the convenience of using metallic money and reduced the cost of evaluating it. But over time, it became common for the certifying authority—the prince, the king, or the government—to abuse its authority by forcing people to accept inferior coinage.

The first coins to be minted date from antiquity. In modern times, every civilized country has minted and circulated a variety of gold or silver coins. When the constitution for the United States was written, it simply recognized the monetary standard that had already been established by popular usage. That happened to be the Spanish milled "dollar." Spanish dollars were silver coins that circulated widely throughout the American colonies. This fact was acknowledged by Thomas Jefferson in his treatise *Notes on the Establishment of a Money Unit, and of a Coinage for the United States*. Jefferson stated that "The unit or dollar is a known coin and the most familiar of all to the mind of the people. It is already adopted from south to north."

These Spanish dollar coins, however, were not uniform in weight or fineness. Dollar coins issued at different times varied slightly from one another. To complete the task of defining the monetary unit for the United States in a way that would not disturb commerce, a committee was commissioned to survey the money stock and assay a representative sampling of Spanish dollar coins so that the American dollar would closely approximate those coins already in circulation. This was easily accomplished and it was quickly settled that the United States dollar should be defined as a silver coin containing 371.25 grains of fine silver. Coins were subsequently minted according to that specification along with gold coins valued in dollars. As the country developed, various expedients were implemented to make money more abundant. These measures, unfortunately, were also used to concentrate economic and political power into fewer hands, as we have already described.

SYMBOLIC MONEY

The simplest form of symbolic money is the "warehouse receipt" or "claim check" for goods on deposit somewhere. A prime example is the grain bank receipts that have been issued at various times and places. In ancient Egypt, as in some African countries today, a farmer might bring his grain crop to a central warehouse and receive receipts for his grain. These receipts might then be exchanged in payment for other goods and services—and when issued in conveniently small denominations, might serve as a general medium of exchange within the region. The holder of the paper notes then has the option of presenting the notes at the warehouse and obtaining the grain they represent.

Paper notes that are redeemable for gold or silver coins are another example of symbolic currency. The general acceptability of symbolic money derives from the fact that it can be redeemed by the holder on demand for the amount of the commodity that it represents. The shift from direct exchange of commodities to the exchange of notes or tokens representing claims to commodities was a sort of half-step that prepared the way for the next evolutionary step. Figure 1 depicts the process of creating symbolic money on the basis of deposits of gold.

THE SECOND EVOLUTIONARY STEP—FROM COMMODITY MONEY TO CREDIT MONEY

The second evolutionary step, what I call *the great monetary transformation*, was the shift from metallic money (commodity money) and "claim check" money (symbolic money) to *credit money*. This transformational development provided a major leap forward in the potential efficacy of exchange media—but unfortunately, it also opened the door for greater abuse. The failure to distinguish between the different kinds of paper money that came into circulation caused much confusion and enabled subtle forms of cheating to proliferate, as we will explain. For now, let us just say that the important question to be answered with regard to any piece of paper currency is "what does the paper represent?" Not all paper is created equal.

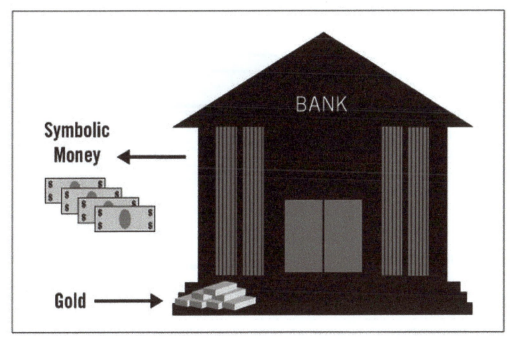

Figure 1 *Bank Notes Issued as Symbolic Money* The first bank notes were symbolic money. They were warehouse receipts for gold or silver on deposit.

Credit money initially took the form of paper banknotes issued independently by various banks; later on, it took the form of bank "deposits" against which checks could be drawn, i.e., what have been called *demand deposits* or, in Europe, *sight deposits.* In either case, whether it takes the form of paper notes or demand deposits, credit money is essentially a promise to pay—what Americans call an IOU. By Withers's account, the introduction of the banknote was the first step in the development of the machinery for "manufacturing credit." As he describes it, "Some ingenious goldsmith conceived the epoch-making notion of giving notes not only to those who had deposited metal, but to those who came to borrow it, and so founded modern banking." Withers's view of credit money is one of "mutual indebtedness" between the banker and his customer. The customer would give the banker his promissory note or mortgage (the customer's debt to the banker) in return for the banker's notes (the banker's debt to the customer), which also carried a promise to pay gold. This process is depicted in Figure 2.

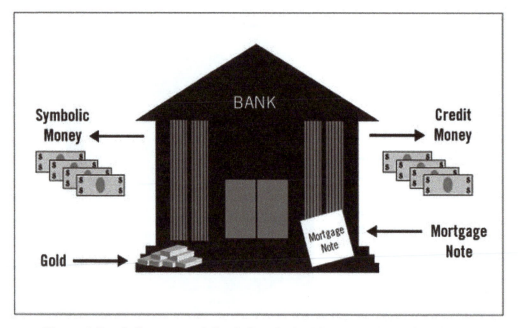

Figure 2 _Bank Creation of Both Symbolic Money and Credit Money_
Banks issued two different kinds of money but they did not distinguish
between them, and few people realized it. The same identical bank notes
were issued to represent both symbolic money and credit money.

But did that "ingenious goldsmith" intend to revolutionize money, or was he
perpetrating a fraud? The prevalent mindset, at that time, considered money
to be gold or silver held on deposit. When the banker issued notes in amounts
greater than the amount of metal in his vault and made all notes redeemable
on demand for metal, the stage was set for trouble.

TWO DISTINCT KINDS OF MONEY—FRACTIONAL RESERVE BANKING

This situation became problematic because now there were two different kinds
of paper money being issued into circulation, the one a "claim check" for gold
on deposit and the other a credit instrument issued on the basis of a promise
to pay and backed by some other form of collateral assets such as merchandise
inventories or real property, _yet both were redeemable for gold._ This "fractional
reserve system," as it came to be known, was problematic from the start.
Whenever people, for any reason, lost confidence in a bank or began to have
doubts about the bank's ability to redeem their notes, there would be a "bank
run." Those who got there first got the gold. When a bank's stores of gold

were exhausted, it would have to close its doors, sometimes never to reopen. At times, when there was a sagging confidence in the banking system as a whole, bank panics became generalized and widespread. Many perfectly sound banks were put out of business because their supply of gold was inadequate to redeem any substantial portion of their issue of banknotes. In the classic film *It's a Wonderful Life*, actor Jimmy Stewart dramatically explains to the people how their money resides not in the bank's vault but in the homes and businesses of their neighbors, perfectly sound collateral the value of which would eventually become liquid again as people repaid their loans.

Those who have decried the issuance of *paper* money have had good reason to do so, but they have also failed to recognize that it is not the paper that is problematic; it is what the paper represents. Paper money that is properly issued on the basis of sound collateral can be a perfectly sound and legitimate medium of exchange. It cannot be too greatly stressed that, as we have already shown, one of the most fundamental problems with paper money historically was the fact that *both* symbolic paper and credit paper were made redeemable for gold. But that problem was compounded by another, more fundamental error—the frequent issuance of paper money on an improper basis often featuring collateral having questionable value. Such worthless collateral, which might be a promissory note, was (like a fraudulent check) often referred to as a "kite."

It is important to realize that those who would have us revert to commodity money like gold and silver do so because they see no other way of imposing discipline upon the powers that have gained control over the process of money creation and allocation, namely bankers and politicians. But by understanding the fundamental nature of modern money as credit, it becomes possible to liberate and perfect it, and to avoid throwing out the more evolved credit money "baby" with the "bath water" of perverse centralization of power.

Another aspect of the money problem was, and is, the manipulation of the supply of credit money by the banking interests operating under the aegis of central governments. By first making credit abundant, then restricting its supply, they can induce people and businesses to borrow and then force them into bankruptcy and foreclosure. The "subprime" mortgage crisis that developed during 2007 and 2008 is a conspicuous example of this. That crisis developed out of the prior inordinate expansion of credit by the banking system on the basis of inflated real estate values. The banks created the real estate "bubble" by lending on (initially) easy terms and low interest rates to unqualified borrowers. Later, when higher interest rates kicked in, many were unable to pay.

REDEEMABILITY ABANDONED

Eventually, the redeemability feature of money was abandoned. In stages, silver and gold were officially demonetized. Now virtually all of the money in circulation is credit money, created by banks when they make loans. This money exists not as banknotes, but in the form of "deposits" in bank accounts. We see then that the problem of the scarcity of conventional money, which at first consisted of gold and silver, was alleviated by the introduction of a new kind of payment medium—credit. This credit was manifested on one side of the bank's ledger (asset) as the borrower's promissory note, and on the other side (liability) as paper currency notes, which were the banker's IOU, as depicted in Figure 3. Giving those early bankers the benefit of the doubt, one can argue that it was first necessary for the community to develop sufficient confidence in this form of money to accept it as a form of payment, and that making the new (credit) money redeemable for the old (gold) money was necessary to building that sort of confidence. Others will argue that making both kinds of money redeemable caused more harm than good to the credibility of paper money generally.

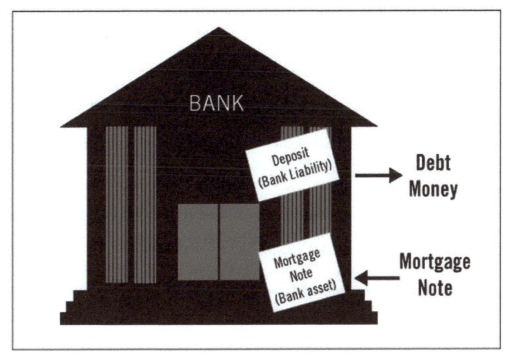

Figure 3 *The Creation of Bank "Debt Money" as Deposits* Banks now issue only debt money, not as notes, but in the form of bank "deposits" when a "loan" is granted.

Be that as it may, the evolutionary step from metallic (commodity) money to credit money was accompanied by much confusion, abuse, and discomfort. The problem stemmed, as we've said, from the concurrent circulation of two different kinds of money and the general failure to distinguish between them. Was a paper banknote merely a claim check for gold held on deposit in the bank's vault, or was it money in itself, a credit instrument backed by some other form of value (a lien against physical inventories of goods, a mortgage on a farm or factory, etc.)?

The problems that arose from the concurrent circulation of both symbolic money and credit money might have been avoided if a clear distinction between them had been made from the beginning and the redeemability feature had been explicitly limited. This, in fact, was proven by the operation of Scottish banks during the early part of the nineteenth century. During that period, notes issued by the Scottish banks gave the banks the option of delaying gold redemption for a certain period of time according to the availability of gold.

These banks became known for their strength and stability and their notes were readily accepted at face value despite this "gold option clause." Banknotes issued on the basis of valuable assets (proper collateral) have proven to be just as sound and acceptable an exchange medium as precious metal coins, without their physical quantity limitations and inconvenience of their transfer. The redeemability feature was carried over during the period when it was thought that public confidence required it. History has shown that redeemability could be readily dispensed with, and credit money has become universally acceptable in its own right.

The point is worth reiterating: Credit money is a legitimate form of money that represents a great improvement over symbolic money that is redeemable for gold or silver. Under the current monetary regime the control of credit by the banking cartel has made it an instrument of power causing great social harm. Nonetheless, the advantages of credit money can be more fully realized as we develop ways to liberate ourselves from conventional banking institutions and political forms of money.

CHECKS AND CHECKABLE DEPOSITS DISPLACE THE USE OF BANKNOTES

Beginning around the mid-nineteenth century, bank deposits and the use of checks to make payments came to predominate over the hand-to-hand transfer of banknotes. Withers describes how this practice arose in response to attempts by the British government to restrict the issuance of banknotes representing credit money and to maintain the note-issuing monopoly in the hands of the Bank of England. In an attempt to address the frequent abuses by issuing banks, which caused recurrent bank failures, the British Parliament passed the Bank Act of 1844. This act prohibited all banks except the Bank of England from issuing banknotes and required that any subsequent issuance of notes by the Bank of England must be based on metal, not on securities. It was an attempt to make the bank note "a mere bullion certificate," i.e., a warehouse receipt for gold held on deposit. While the intention of this law may have been good, the effects could have been extremely problematic for trade and industry because it restricted the supply of exchange media.

Withers points out that:

> If the apparent intentions of the Act of 1844 had been carried out, been possible at all, must have been accompanied by the heaping up of a vast

amount of gold in the Bank's vault. But its intentions were evaded by the commercial community, which had already accepted the advantages of a currency based on mutual indebtedness between itself and the banks (credit money). The commercial community ceased to circulate bank-notes under the new restrictions, developing the use for daily cash transactions of a credit instrument which had already acquired some popularity, namely, a draft or bill on its bankers payable on demand and now commonly called a cheque. The drawing of cheques was not in any way limited by the Act of 1844, and the cheque was in many ways a more convenient form of currency than the bank-note.... The use of the cheque, however, involves the element of belief to a much greater extent than that of the bank-note.

Thus we see another instance in which "necessity is the mother of invention." Since a check is not money but merely an order to pay money, anyone who accepts a check must first ascertain the credibility of both the drawer of the check and the bank upon which it is drawn. Does the drawer of the check actually have an account with the stated bank, and is that account not overdrawn? Does the bank on which the check is drawn actually exist, and is it solvent? Despite these risks, and despite the fact that checks were not legal tender, their use became ever more popular. In Withers's words, "the cheque has had to fight its way to its present supremacy without this advantage [of legal tender status], and to drive gold and notes out of circulation...in spite of the fact that they were legal tender and it was not. This it was enabled to do by its safety and convenience and the power of the drawer to hedge it about with restrictions."

The convenience of the check is obvious to those of us who grew up using it, but considering the risks described above, what makes it safe, and what are the restrictions that Withers speaks of? First off, it can be legally negotiated (cashed or deposited) only by the payee. Unlike banknotes (which anyone can spend) a check, if it is lost or stolen, cannot easily be cashed or spent by the finder or thief. In addition, it can be made out for the exact amount due and after it is cancelled it is returned to the drawer to serve as a record and receipt for payment.

Many monetary reformers today still believe that money, to be sound, must be fully backed by gold or silver and be redeemable on demand. But this would be a step backward to a more primitive medium of exchange, and would unnecessarily throttle the exchange process. The limited supply of whatever commodities might serve as money would limit the amount of trading that could take place with disastrous consequences for the economy. The reasons for this will become clear as we proceed. The answer to the abusive issuance and circulation of credit money lies not in turning back the clock and reverting to more primitive forms, but in perfecting the superior form, credit money, within the arena of free competition. The biggest challenge then is to find ways of transcending the political money system that has gained a virtual monopoly on credit worldwide.

The general lack of understanding of the real nature of money and the proper basis for credit money has often caused the political debate to run askew, leading many well-intended reformers to inadvertently restrict the supply of exchange media in an attempt to remedy abusive banking practices. Such was the case during the Jackson era (roughly, the second third of the nineteenth century). In the "Bank War" that we described in Chapter 4, President Andrew Jackson rightly put an end to the extreme privilege and power of the Second Bank of the United States, but at the same time he also adopted a restrictive "hard money" policy. Fortunately, the proliferation of banks and the easy availability of credit during this "free banking" period, while sometimes flawed, enabled a great expansion of industry and commerce.

The real argument is not between gold versus paper, but between *commodity* money versus *credit* money. To posit the argument as between specie and paper misses the point by confusing the physical manifestation or form of money with the substance of money. It is the *basis of issue* of money that is all-important. Paper money can represent a "claim check" or "warehouse receipt" for gold on deposit (symbolic money), or it can represent the value inherent in particular collateral assets against which credit is monetized (credit money). Under the original fractional reserve banking system, these two were confused and intermingled, making trouble inevitable. So long as both claim check money and credit money were redeemable for specie one could expect periodic bank runs and panics.

The supply of commodities like gold and silver is limited by natural factors, and the cost of increasing such supply (by the process of mining, refining, and coining—or even by taking it as plunder) is very great. Furthermore, it is destructive to the environment. How does it make sense to dig gold out of one hole (a mine) only to bury it again in another (vault)? Gold has very little use value aside from ornamentation—its desirability derives primarily from its historical "exchange value." In times of financial uncertainty, gold may serve as an effective *savings medium* by hedging against the effects of inflation of legal tender currency. It can also provide portability of wealth for refugees, as well as some measure of financial privacy. Gold might serve to define a measure of value, but it will not return as a primary payment medium unless there is a major breakdown of civilization. The expansion of credit, on the other hand, can be achieved at very low cost, and its quantity is limited only by the collective capacity to produce and the aggregate value of the goods and services that people wish to exchange. *By enabling every producer to create—within reasonable limits—the credit money needed to satisfy their needs for goods and services, it is possible to have a flexible-yet-sound means of facilitating exchange.*

HOW CREDIT MONEY MALFUNCTIONS

A multitude of problems derive from abuse of the credit creation function. The great leap forward that credit money represented was, and still is, perverted by a financial regime that centralizes power and concentrates wealth. The monopolistic control over credit, exercised through a banking cartel armed with government-granted privilege, allows wealth to be extracted from producer clients and, despite the trappings of democracy, the control of governments to be maintained in the hands of a few. Credit is allocated on a biased basis to favored clients, including central governments, which distorts both the system of economic rewards and the exercise of political power. Under this regime, the people's own credit is privatized and "loaned" back to them at interest. The enormous benefits that credit money makes possible can be realized only if credit is created democratically on a proper value basis by the people themselves. What that basis should be and how it should be done will be addressed subsequently.

Greco claims that "many monetary reformers today still believe that money, to be sound, must be fully backed by gold or silver" (page 181). Using the Internet—both news sources and the sites sponsored by politicians, candidates, PACs, and independent political opinion sites—explore the contemporary rhetoric of the gold standard. Who is making this case, and what else is a part of their political platform? Are there any consistencies that seem interesting or significant?

The language of currency, as Greco points out, is notoriously misleading and anachronistic: "deposit," "loan," and similar terms have become purely metaphorical, having long lost their concrete referents. In a paragraph, try to describe an economic transaction—buying your textbooks, maybe—in perfectly literal terms.

MAJOR ASSIGNMENTS

MAJOR ASSIGNMENT #1
LIVING ON $126 ($107) DOLLARS A DAY / LIVING ON $30 ($27) A DAY

BACKGROUND

The median household annual income in the United States for a single person is $46,000, or, roughly $126 per day. Daily living might seem easy on this amount, but for most this amount is reduced by recurring debt payments, in addition to shelter and food, and these numbers do not include income tax. The average American carries $3,752 in credit card debt and $21,000 in student loans; to pay off these debts in a year, the borrower would need to pay $325 per month on the credit cards and $243 on student loans. We can recalculate the daily allowance, then, to $107.

A single person at the poverty level, though, earns an annual income of $10,800 or lower, making their daily income only $30. And in the rest of the world it can be much, much lower—in some countries, the equivalent of just pennies a day. For those at the poverty line in the United States, debt has exploded in the last twenty years, with what is called "hardship debt" (40% or more of annual income) affecting up to 75% of those at the poverty line. Let's place the service on this debt at $3 per day for a total of $27 per day.

ASSIGNMENT

This assignment involves inquiry into the practicalities of daily finances, something of which one must be aware to have even a basic level of financial literacy. For this assignment you must plan out your day financially, both at the median income level and at the poverty line. Assuming that you have start-up costs to put a deposit on a place to live and to seek some kind of employment— much like Ehrenreich (page 95) did when she began her experiment—you will need to find a job, a place to live, and transportation in the place you would like to live. Then, calculate an average day's income and expenses. Provide a menu for the day, including its costs. Take into account various kinds of insurance you must pay (auto, for example), as well as telecommunication costs (assume that you are still making payments on a device and a plan). Entertainment will definitely be a consideration if during this day you intend to see a movie or take in a ballgame, but you will, for some expenses, have to figure a monthly cost and divide by 30 days to find the daily expense. If you intend to have cable television or internet, for instance, you will have a daily entertainment cost even if you don't seek an outside activity.

In the first section of your paper, contextualize the relative income and relative expenses between median income earners and earners at the poverty line. The next section will be your daily plans and expenses. In the concluding section you should reflect on the benefits and difficulties of living within your means and how those benefits and difficulties differ between the two income groups. Finally, reflect on how you expect to live upon graduation, what financial situation you anticipate, and how your expectations may have changed by completing this project.

RESEARCH

Websites such as the Bureau of Labor Statistics, the White House's Office of Budget, and the Department of Health and Human Services will be invaluable to find statistics on income and expenses. Websites such as Craigslist, Monster, and various online classifieds will help you to find jobs, shelter, and transportation, as may newspapers local to your chosen area, many of which are also available online. You might think about going to a grocery or convenience store in person to price food. If you decide to own a house or condominium, there are many mortgage calculators online (assume you could afford a 5% down payment).

MULTIMODAL OPTIONS

Unless your instructor requires a specific type of presentation, you may think about the ways in which visual components and/or hyperlinks might convey your final conclusions more effectively to an audience. An electronic document or PowerPoint presentation might be more effective than a printed paper. You may incorporate numerical charts into the page layout so that readers may easily visualize the differences and similarities you've discovered. Beyond that, you could create this as a hypertext, a webpage with links to relevant articles, even maps of your neighborhood with the distance you have to travel to and from work. You could include bus or train schedules. You could include recipes of the meals you will eat. You could paste in pictures of the house or apartment you will live in, a picture of the car you will drive, your place of employment, a picture of your boss—anything that will help your audience imagine the life you might live under the budget constraints given in the assignment.

MAJOR ASSIGNMENT #2
NARRATIVE: WHAT DO YOU VALUE AND
HOW DO YOU VALUE IT?

BACKGROUND

Money is often, but not always, a consideration when assessing the value of the material items in our lives. From a quilt handed down through the generations to a new Ford Mustang, we use different kinds of systems to determine the value of the things we own. MP Dunleavey, in "Buy Yourself Less Stuff," writes about the "hedonic treadmill" where consumers buy more and more with less and less satisfaction, and George F. Will in "A Lexus in Every Garage" articulates the ways in which some items have "positional" value. This is not to mention classic ideas of use and exchange value inherent in various economic schools of thought.

ASSIGNMENT

In this assignment you are invited to tell the story of a material good that you care about. How did you come to possess it? Why do you keep it? On the contrary, if it applies: How did you come to lose it or give it away? Further: What have you wanted and denied yourself, and why do you refrain from acquiring it? For this assignment you should discuss the value of this item and the systems of value that you apply to it. What is the item worth to you? Why? Are your systems of value externally valid; that is, would others share your criteria? Can you critique your valuation system?

CONSIDERATIONS WHEN WRITING NARRATIVES

Narratives tell stories, and as such they share certain characteristics. Generally, they have characters, settings, and actions. When you are thinking about the narrative aspects of your essay, you should consider these specifics. Who is the main character and what is that character like? If you are the main character, how can you share the relevant parts of your personality effectively with your audience? What happens in the story; what is the tension, and how does it resolve? Where does the action happen? Remember that it is very likely that your readers have not met the characters, nor have they been in the setting you are using. A good narrative uses pertinent details to bring the story to life for the reader.

MAJOR ASSIGNMENT #3
EXPLORATION ESSAY

BACKGROUND

Each field of study or "discipline" in higher education narrows its inquiry to its specific concerns: sociology focuses on group activity, action, and thought; physics, the world of matter and energy; ethnic studies, the outlook and treatment of diverse cultures and subcultures. Economics, though, besides being its own field, is a pervasive concern for many people and groups. Money is important, and as a result, many different fields of study have their own perspectives on value, exchange, and financial behaviors. Someone in the field of physics, for instance, might look at the economic realities of paying for expensive machinery to do experiments with and how economics limits scientific discovery. Similarly, someone in ethnic studies might look at class structures among different sub-groups within a larger ethnic class. In this book, Zelizer writes about how financial issues affect groups of women in different classes; Franklin ties money to religion and faith. Any conversation spread this widely across disciplinary viewpoints is likely to be fractious, as many different voices assert many different arguments. "Discourse communities" are groups of people who communicate with one another within particular rules: simply put, they discuss certain things in certain ways. They have different rules of evidence, different jargon, and field-specific language (compare an article in the *Journal of the American Medical Association* to an article in *College English* to see this in action).

ASSIGNMENT

This assignment asks you to survey the discussion of money across discourse communities. Ideally, you will look at your own major to find a starting point (if you haven't decided on a major, you can take this opportunity to explore one). What are the economic issues at the forefront of that discourse community? How do professionals in that community talk about the issue, and what conflicts (or what other discourse communities) do they come up against? Each discipline will have specific concerns and ask specific questions. The idea of this assignment is not to present an argument but to survey arguments, not to present just two sides but to present a plethora of conflicting positions on a complex and important issue.

INVENTION STRATEGIES AND RESEARCH

To begin, choose the disciplinary view you want to explore (you already know that the topic is money). Generate a list of questions asked by this field of study. This list will be a good starting point for narrowing the topic; indeed, if you were just to use "money" as the topic, you could be writing this essay for years before you thoroughly covered the topic. Settle on a compelling and controversial economic issue within your discipline. For instance, early childhood education majors might explore the arguments surrounding the use of federal stimulus money to boost the wages of daycare professionals (an argument forwarded in 2009). After you have the disciplinary topic, brainstorm, research, and talk with your classmates about various approaches to the topic. You might also talk to your professors and instructors or professionals in the field who will have some perspective (and probably personal and professional ideas) on the topic. Never forget that primary research is a great way to generate knowledge.

MULTIMODAL COMPONENT

A project this multifaceted may be more effectively presented in a multimodal form than as a traditional essay. You could make a hypertext annotated bibliography as you begin this project, especially if you are doing a great deal of internet research (which should include various scholarly databases subscribed to by your library). Your final essay could be a hypertext in which you embed links to articles and websites you are referencing, visually signifying the disciplinary variety represented in your survey. In PowerPoint you could create an impressionistic collage of pictures, graphics, and words that enhance the spoken presentation of your exploration. Often, an audience appreciates more than just bulleted lists of points that you are trying to make.

MAJOR ASSIGNMENT #4
ARGUMENT

BACKGROUND

As you have read through the essays, songs, comics, and excerpts in this book, you have noticed that money touches many, many aspects of our lives. Not only does money determine economic class, it even affects the way we behave, even the way we believe. It determines our choices as much as it reveals our value systems. It has material benefits and ethical consequences. As noted in the introduction, money is both a real, tangible object and a symbolic system that exists by human agreement. It is both a complex entity and an abstract complexity of competing ideas. Depending on one's upbringing, geographical setting, psychology, belief system, group affiliations, even one's generation, gender, and numerous other factors, a person interacts with and thinks about money in very specific and sometimes conflicting ways.

ASSIGNMENT

Write an argumentative essay in which you attempt to persuade or convince a specific audience about an issue involving money. Ideally, you will research the topic broadly (as you did in the Exploratory Essay #3) before you settle on your position. A good argument acknowledges that there are often many sides to an issue rather than positing the issue as merely either/or. As well as evidence to back up your claims, an argument of value, ethics, or priority particularly requires the establishment of premises that logically support its conclusions. Use premises and evidence that will be persuasive to your specific audience.

If your instructor allows it, you might use the Exploratory Essay as a precursor to this essay.

POSSIBLE TOPICS BASED ON SELECTIONS IN THIS BOOK

- Demonetization of creative products and virtual or alternate economies —Lanier, Greco

- The role of money in religious practice and philosophy—Franklin

- The cost of the public good—Picht

- The plight of the impoverished—Foster, Scalzi

- The inequality of wealth—Ariely, McLean, Bernstein

- Redistribution of wealth—Roosevelt, Stiglitz, Wolff

- Virtual purchases and relationships—Dibbell, Lanier

- Money and corruption—McLean

- Gender issues and money—Perle, Ehrenreich, Zelizer

- Altruism, Asceticism, Hedonism—McCoy, Mos Def

- Value of labor—Bernstein, Lanier, Ehrenreich, Roosevelt

- Digital piracy—Lanier, Dibbell

CONSIDERATIONS WHEN WRITING ARGUMENTS

Academic arguments, be they in the humanities, social sciences, or natural sciences, tend toward objectivity and neutrality (at least as much as they can, given that objectivity and neutrality are complicated ideas). The writer wants to present evidence that is persuasive to the audience while acknowledging the strengths of counterarguments. Your case should be laid out with this in mind. Although recent research using MRI machines suggests that people make decisions on an emotional level first and then rationalize the choice in the conscious mind, academic arguments tend to follow the procedures of the courts—everyone gets his or her say, and everyone is treated more or less fairly.

MAJOR ASSIGNMENT #5
SATIRE

BACKGROUND

Satire is generally defined as the use of irony—literally saying the opposite of the message one intends to convey—to expose the foolishness, recklessness, and irrationality of the human condition, though it is generally aimed at those people and institutions that embody those very follies and vices. The most famous satire in English is "A Modest Proposal" by Jonathan Swift, in which the speaker proposes that Irish peasants sell their infants as food products for consumption by English landowners. Swift certainly wasn't seriously advocating cannibalism but merely pointing out the harsh conditions under which the Irish lived and the English landowners' complicity in the situation. Today, *South Park* and *The Colbert Report* may represent the truest satires in our popular culture. Indeed, Colbert embodies the irony central to satire: he portrays a conservative political pundit whose every word critiques conservative political ideology. In this book you have read two satires: one from *The Onion* and one from Joseph Heller's *Catch-22*. Heller's novel satirizes free market capitalism by showing mess captain Milo Minderbinder's business success finally leading to the Germans paying him to have his own squadron bombed. The irony comes from Milo's justification for his actions, attitudes Heller is clearly critiquing. While *The Onion*, Heller, and even Swift lampoon economic attitudes in the past, a good recent example is the "Margaritaville" episode of South Park, which can be found at the following URL: (http://www.southparkstudios.com/full-episodes/s13e03-margaritaville)/

ASSIGNMENT

Write a satire that exposes some foolishness, recklessness, or irrationality in the economic system or in the human use of money. Given the last few years, there are certainly many targets: bankers, politicians, political parties, home buyers, real estate agents, the rich, the poor, or individual consumers, to name a few. One could turn to reality TV and find spendthrifts and tightwads in the extreme, as well as home shopping hawkers, house hunters, house builders, and various causes soliciting donations. Choose your topic, think through your attitude, and then seek a way to flip it over into irony.

INVENTION STRATEGIES

Discovering a topic for the satire is one of the hardest parts of the assignment. Collaborative brainstorming sessions are helpful for this. The writing staff on any comedy show bounce ideas off each other and work with one another to develop sketches and jokes. Groups of writers should band together to have free-for-all sessions where individuals throw out ideas while others in the group add to and modify the ideas.

The idea is to generate a target and then an ironic, even outlandish, angle on the target. For instance, the South Park episode ultimately targets officials at the Treasury who, we find, make decisions based on the movement of decapitated chickens. The difficulty in writing any satire is its indirect nature: Saying one thing that really means another while still conveying the writer's true intention (indeed, there are many examples throughout the history of satire where readers took the writer at his or her word). Your peer group may help you determine whether you're hitting or missing the mark.

You must also decide what genre you will use. Satire is a strategy but not a genre in and of itself. Heller and the writers of South Park use narrative; Swift uses the argumentative essay; *The Onion* writers and Stephen Colbert use journalism.

MULTIMODAL COMPONENT

If you wish to take your project off the paper, a narrative satire can be presented by short film or Flash animation. If you use journalism, you could present a fake news report or talk show sketch. Brainstorm with your group for ways you can help one another—as extras, actors, or camera operators, perhaps—enhance the presentation of your final project.

FILMOGRAPHY

DOCUMENTARIES

Bling: Consequences and Repercussions (2005)
Born Rich (2003)
Capitalism: A Love Story (2009)
The End of Poverty? (2008)
Enron: The Smartest Guys in the Room (2005)
I.O.U.S.A. (2008)
Inside Job (2010)
Maxed Out (2006)
The Shock Doctrine (2007)
Wal-Mart: The High Cost of Low Prices (2005)
What Would Jesus Buy? (2007)

COMEDIES & DRAMAS

Boiler Room (2000)
Brewster's Millions (1985)
The Company Men (2010)
Easy Living (1937)
The Exterminating Angel (1962)
Glengarry Glen Ross (1992)
The Grapes of Wrath (1940)
Indecent Proposal (1993)
Mr. Deeds Goes to Town (1936)
Slumdog Millionaire (2008)
Trading Places (1983)

Up In The Air (2009)
Wall Street (1987)
Wall Street: Money Never Sleeps (2010)

WORKS CITED

Ariely, Dan. *The Upside of Irrationality: The Unexpected Benefits of Defying Logic at Work and at Home*. New York: Harper, 2010. Print.

Bernstein, Jared. *Crunch: Why Do I Feel So Squeezed: (And Other Unsolved Economic Mysteries)*. San Francisco: Barret-Koehler, 2008. Print.

Dibbell, Julian. "The Decline and Fall of an Ultra Rich Online Gaming Empire." *Wired*. N.p., 24 Nov. 2008. Web. 29 July 2011. Path: www. wired.com.

Dunleavey, MP. *Money Can Buy Happiness: How To Spend To Get the Life You Want*. New York: Broadway Books, 2007. Print.

Ehrenreich, Barbara. *Nickel and Dimed: On (Not) Getting By in America*. New York: Owl/Holt, 2001. Print.

Foster, Stephen C. "Hard Times Come Again No More." Public Domain, 1854.

Franklin, Robert M. "The Gospel of Bling." *Sojourner's* 36.1 Jan. (2007): 18-44. Print.

Greco, Thomas H. *The End of Money and the Future of Civilization*. White River Junction, VT: Chelsea Green Publishing, 2009. Print.

Heller, Joseph. *Catch-22*. New York: Simon and Schuster, 1961. Print.

Lanier, Jaron. *You Are Not a Gadget*. New York: Vintage, 2010. Print.

McCoy, Travis L. "Billionaire." *Lazarus*. Perf. Bruno Mars. Fueled By Ramen, New York, 2010. CD.

McLean, Bethany and Peter Elkind. *The Smartest Guys in the Room: The Amazing Rise and Scandalous Fall of Enron*. New York: Penguin, 2003. Print.

Mos Def. "Got." *Black on Both Sides*. Priority Records, Los Angeles, 1999. CD.

Perle, Liz. *Money: A Memoir*. New York: Holt, 2006. Print.

Picht, Jim. "Burning Down the House: Beck and Olbermann Are Both Wrong about the Cranick Fire." *The Washington Times*, 7 Oct. 2010. Web. 29 July 2011. Path: http://communities.washingtontimes.com.

Roosevelt, Franklin D. "Message on the State of the Union." 1944.

Scalzi, John. "Being Poor." *Whatever*. N.p., 3 Sept. 2005. Web. 29 July 2011. <http://whatever.scalzi.com/2005/09/03/being-poor/>.

Stiglitz, Joseph E. "Of the 1%, by the 1%, for the 1%." *Vanity Fair* May 2011: 126-29. Print.

"U.S. Economy Grinds To Halt As Nation Realizes Money Just A Symbolic, Mutually Shared Illusion." *The Onion*. N.p., 16 Feb. 2010. Web. 29 July 2011. Path: http://www.theonion.com/articles.

Watterson, Bill. "Calvin & Hobbes." Cartoon. *Andrews McMeel Publishing* 10 July 1987. Print.

---. "Calvin & Hobbes." Cartoon. *Andrews McMeel Publishing* 27 August 1992. Print.

Will, George F. "A Lexus in Every Garage." *The Washington Post*. N.p., 11 Oct. 2007. Web. 29 July 2011. Path: http://www.washingtonpost.com.

Wolff, Edward N. *Top Heavy: The Increasing Inequality of Wealth in America and What Can Be Done About It*. New York: The New Press, 2002. Print.

Zelizer, Viviana A. *The Social Meaning of Money*. New York: Basic Books, 1994. Print.